NC

ISIS AND SYRIA

The new global
war on terror

About the author
Phyllis Bennis is a Fellow of the Institute for Policy Studies and of the Transnational Institute in Amsterdam. She writes and speaks widely on US wars and foreign policy and is the author of numerous books, including *Inside Israel-Palestine: the conflict explained* (New Internationalist). She plays a leading role in US and global movements against wars and occupation.

About the New Internationalist
New Internationalist is an award-winning, independent media co-operative. Our aim is to inform, inspire and empower people to build a fairer, more sustainable planet.

We publish a global justice magazine and a range of books, both distributed worldwide. We have a vibrant online presence and run ethical online shops for our customers and other organizations.

- **Independent media:** we're free to tell it like it is – our only obligation is to our readers and the subjects we cover.

- **Fresh perspectives:** our in-depth reporting and analysis provide keen insights, alternative perspectives and positive solutions for today's critical global justice issues.

- **Global grassroots voices:** we actively seek out and work with grassroots writers, bloggers and activists across the globe, enabling unreported (and under-reported) stories to be heard.

NONONSENSE

ISIS AND SYRIA

The new global
war on terror

Phyllis Bennis

New Internationalist

NONONSENSE

ISIS and Syria
The new global war on terror

Published in 2016 in an updated edition by
New Internationalist Publications Ltd
The Old Music Hall
106-108 Cowley Road
Oxford OX4 1JE, UK
newint.org

First published in North America in 2015 as 'Understanding ISIS and the
New Global War on Terror: A Primer' by Interlink Books, 46 Crosby Street,
Northampton, MA, 01060-1804, USA.
interlinkbooks.com

Cover design: Juha Sorsa
Design concept: Andrew Smith, asmithcompany.co.uk

Series editor: Chris Brazier
Series design: Juha Sorsa

Printed and bound in Great Britain by Bell & Bain Ltd, Glasgow
who hold environmental accreditation ISO 14001.

MIX
Paper from
responsible sources
FSC® C007785
FSC
www.fsc.org

British Library Cataloguing-in-Publication Data.
A catalogue record for this book is available from the British Library.

ISBN 978-1-78026-312-0
(ISBN ebook 978-1-78026-313-7)

Contents

Introduction

The rise of Islamic State in Iraq and Syria, or ISIS, and the US war against it have exploded into a regional and global conflagration. Once again, civilians are paying the price for both extremist attacks and US wars.

When ISIS swept across northern Syria and northwestern Iraq in June 2014, occupying cities and towns and imposing its draconian version of Islam on terrified populations, to many around the world it looked like something that had popped up out of nowhere. This was not the case, but the complicated interweaving of players, places, and alliances make understanding ISIS seem almost impossible. Yet ISIS has a traceable past, a history and a political trajectory grounded in movements, organizations, governments, and political moments that form a long story in the Middle East: from Saudi Arabia to al-Qaeda, from the US invasion and occupation of Iraq to the Arab Spring, regime change in Libya and the chaos of Syria's civil war.

The US war against ISIS, President Obama's iteration of George Bush's much-heralded and long-failed 'global war on terror', presents us with an equally complex set of paradoxes and contradictions. The US is fighting against ISIS alongside Iran and the Iranian-backed Baghdad government in Iraq, and fighting in Syria against ISIS alongside (sort of) the Iranian-backed and US-opposed government in Damascus. And all the while, the US and its Arab Gulf allies are arming and paying a host of largely unaccountable, predominantly Sunni militias that are fighting against the Syrian government and fighting – sort of – against ISIS. Meanwhile, in Iraq, the Iranian government is arming and training a host of largely unaccountable, predominantly Shi'a militias that are fighting against ISIS and – sort of – alongside the US-backed Iraqi government.

It's a mess.

That's why this book came to be written. It's designed to help readers sort out the history and the players, identify who's doing what to whom, who's on what side, and most of all, figure out what we can do to help stop the killing. That's why the last questions in the book are perhaps the most important – what would alternative policies toward ISIS, toward the region, toward war and peace, actually look like? What can we all do to bring those alternative approaches into the light of day?

For more than a century, US policy in the Middle East has been rooted largely in maintaining access to and control of oil. For roughly three-quarters of a century, in addition to its oil agenda, US policy has had a Cold War-driven strategic interest in stability and US bases to challenge competitors and project power. And, for almost half a century, US policy has been built on a triple play of oil plus stability plus Israel.

While each component of this triplet played the dominant role at different times, overall US interests in the region remained constant. But some changes are under way. Oil is still important to the global economy, but as the threat posed by oil's role in global warming becomes better understood and sustainable alternatives continue to emerge, it is less of a factor than it once was. And where it comes from is changing too. The US is producing and exporting more oil than ever, and while the Middle East is still a huge exporter of oil, Africa surpassed the Middle East as a source of US oil imports in 2010.

The US continues to pay more than $3.1 billion every year of taxpayer money to the Israeli military, and continues to provide absolute protection to Israel in the United Nations and elsewhere, assuring that no Israeli officials are held accountable for potential war crimes or human rights violations. But with rising tensions between Washington and Tel Aviv over settlement expansion and especially over Israel's efforts to undermine Washington's negotiations with Iran, President Obama in 2015 for the first time hinted at a shift, indicating that the US might reconsider its grant of absolute impunity to Israel. With public opinion shifting dramatically away from the assumption that Israel can do no wrong, and influential, increasingly mainstream campaigns pushing policymakers in that direction, a real shift in US policy may be on its way. We're not there yet, but change is coming.

That leaves strategic stability, military bases and ability to 'project power' – read: send troops and bombers – as the most important 'national interest' driving US policy in the Middle East. This means that the war on terror, the seemingly permanent US response to instability in the region, is strategically more important – and far more dangerous – than ever.

That war is rooted in the aftermath of the September 11, 2001 attacks – the US invasion of Afghanistan, and especially the 2003 invasion and occupation of Iraq. Twelve years after the invasion of Iraq, several groups of physicians attempted to accomplish what the 'we don't do body counts' Pentagon had long refused to do: calculate the human costs of the US war on terror. In 'Body Count: Casualty Figures After Ten Years of the War on Terror', the Nobel Peace Prize-winning International Physicians for the Prevention of Nuclear War, Physicians for Social Responsibility, and Physicians for Global Survival together reached the staggering conclusion that the war was responsible for the loss of at least 1.3 million lives in Iraq, Afghanistan, and Pakistan from the September 11, 2001 attacks until 2013.

And that total didn't take into account the more than 500,000 Iraqi children killed by US-imposed economic sanctions in the 1990s in the run-up to the war. It didn't take into account the expansion of the wars to Libya and Syria, or include President Obama's expanding drone war in Somalia and Yemen. It didn't take into account the rapidly escalating casualty figures in 2014 and 2015 throughout the theatres of the war on terror. But the shocking death toll is still a vital reality check on those who would assert that somehow the war on terror is 'worth the price', as former Secretary of State Madeleine Albright famously described the death of half a million Iraqi children under sanctions.

This book aims to help probe behind the propaganda, help sort out the facts from the mythology, help figure out what we need to know to build a path away from war as the default option. There may be some duplication between some of the questions, and some sections provide different levels of detail than others. The questions are organized by subject, designed for readers to pick and choose, find a subject of interest and delve into the questions most relevant to that subject, then come back later to other issues.

Inevitably, writing a book like this presents enormous challenges, not least the rapid pace of events. Just when you think you've got most of the region covered, Yemen explodes. Just when you think you've clarified the possibilities and dangers for the Iran nuclear talks, the interim agreement is announced and anti-diplomacy hardliners in Tehran and especially in Washington start their campaigns to undermine it. This is not a full, definitive account of ISIS, its theology, or its strategy. This is an overview, designed to provide a basic understanding so we can move toward identifying and implementing new alternative strategies, instead of war.

Ultimately, that is the reason for this book: to help activists, policymakers, journalists, students – and all the people in their orbit – with the hard task of changing the discourse and turning Western policy around. The basic assumption underlying this book is that you can't bomb extremism – you can only bomb people. And even if some of the people you bomb are extremists, those bombing campaigns cause more extremism, not less. We need to move away from war as an answer to extremism, and instead build a new approach grounded in diplomacy and negotiation, arms embargos and international law, the United Nations, humanitarian assistance and human rights.

Phyllis Bennis
Washington DC

October 2015

1 ISIS

What are the origins of ISIS?

Political Islam in its modern form, as Mahmoud Mamdani states in *Good Muslims, Bad Muslims*, is 'more a domestic product than a foreign import'. It was not, he reminds us, 'bred in isolation... Political Islam was born in the colonial period. But it did not give rise to a terrorist movement until the Cold War.' The Muslim Brotherhood in Egypt was born almost a century ago. Its followers in neighbouring countries contested for power (rarely winning any) with governments across the region. The mobilization against the US-backed Shah in Iran in the 1970s resulted in the establishment of the Islamic Republic of Iran under the leadership of Ayatollah Ruhollah Khomeini in perhaps the most powerful, self-defined Islamic government of the 20th century. But today's movement known as political Islam, with its military mobilizations holding pride of place ahead of its political formations, emerged in its first coherent identity with the US-armed, US-paid, Pakistani-trained *mujahideen* warriors who fought the Soviet troops in Afghanistan from 1979 onwards. Continuing in the post-Vietnam Cold War 1980s, the Afghanistan War ended with the defeat and ultimate collapse of the Soviet Union.

The specific origins of ISIS, also variously known as ISIL, Daesh or the Islamic State, lie in the 2003 US invasion and occupation of Iraq. The country was already in terrible shape, following decades of war (the Iran-Iraq War from 1980-89, then the first US Gulf War in 1991) and a dozen years of crippling economic sanctions imposed in 1990. Even after the first wars, and despite brutal repression of any potential opposition and the long-standing political and economic privileging of the large (20 per cent or so) Sunni minority, the majority of Iraqis lived middle-class lives, including government-provided free healthcare and education, with some of the best medical and scientific institutions in the Arab world. The sanctions, imposed in the name of the United Nations but created and enforced by the US, had shredded much of the social fabric of the once-prosperous, secular, cosmopolitan country. The Pentagon's 'shock and awe' bombing campaign that opened the US invasion destroyed much of Iraq's physical infrastructure, as well as the lives of over 7,000 Iraqi civilians.

How did the 2003 invasion of Iraq affect the growth of ISIS?

Among the first acts of the US-UK occupation were the dissolution of the Iraqi military, the dismantling of the civil service, and the overthrow of Saddam Hussein's ruling Baath Party. All three institutions represented core concentrations of secular nationalist interests in Iraq, and their collapse was part of the reason for the turn toward religious and sectarian identity that began to replace national identity for many Iraqis. At the same time, in all three institutions, particularly at the highest echelons, Sunni Iraqis were more likely to suffer from the loss of income and prestige – since Sunnis held a dispropor-tionate share of top jobs and top positions in the military and the Baath Party. So, right from the beginning, a sectarian strand emerged at the very centre of the rising opposition to the occupation.

Despite the Bush administration's dismissals of the opposition as nothing but Baathist leftovers and foreign fighters, the Iraqi resistance was far broader. Within months of the March 2003 invasion, militias and informal groups of fighters were challenging the US-UK occupation across the country. One of the earliest was al-Qaeda in Iraq or AQI, sometimes known as al-Qaeda in Mesopotamia, a Sunni militia created in 2004 by Abu Mussab al-Zarqawi. He was Jordanian, although it appears most of the early members of AQI were Iraqis.

Al-Zarqawi announced publicly that AQI had pledged loyalty to the leadership of al-Qaeda and specifically to Osama bin Laden. The militia's tactics included bombings and improvised explosive devices (IEDs), as well as reported kidnappings and beheadings. While AQI began with a focus on the US and other coalition forces, aiming to rid Iraq of foreign occupiers, it soon expanded to adopt a more explicitly sectarian agenda, in which the Shi'a-dominated Iraqi government, military and police forces as well as Shi'a civilians were also targeted.

Over the next several years, the forces fighting against the occupation of Iraq became more sectarian, moving toward what would become a bloody civil war fought alongside the resistance to occupation. Beginning in 2006, the US shifted its Iraq strategy, deciding to move away from direct fighting against Sunni anti-occupation fighters and instead to try to co-opt them. The essence of the Sunni Awakening plan was that the US would bankroll Sunni tribal leaders, those who had earlier led the anti-US resistance, paying them off to fight *with* the occupation and US-backed Shi'a-dominated government instead of against them. They would also fight against the Sunni outliers, those who rejected the Awakening movement, which included al-Qaeda in Iraq. And just about the time that the Sunni Awakening was taking hold, al-Qaeda in Iraq changed its name – this time to Islamic State of Iraq, or ISI.

In August 2014, when Iraq's Anbar province had been largely overrun by ISIS, its governor, Ahmed al-Dulaimi, described for the *New York Times* the trajectory of an ISIS leader whom al-Dulaimi had taught in military school. 'It was never clear that he would turn out like that,' al-Dulaimi told the *Times*.

'He was from a simple family, with high morals, but all his brothers went in that direction [becoming jihadists].' After the US invaded Iraq in 2003, al-Dulaimi's former pupil joined al-Qaeda in Iraq and was detained by US forces in 2005. According to al-Dulaimi: 'We continue

to live with the consequences of the decision to disband
Saddam's army... All of these guys got religious after
2003... Surely, ISIS benefits from their experience.'

Who is Abu Bakr al-Baghdadi and what was his role in the rise of ISIS?

In June 2006 al-Zarqawi was killed by US bombs.
According to some sources, four months later Abu Bakr
al-Baghdadi was announced as the new leader of AQI,
having been released from 10 months or so in the US-run
Bucca prison in Iraq. Other sources claim that al-Baghdadi
spent as much as five years in the US prison, and that after
the death of al-Zarqawi, AQI was taken over by a different
person with a similar name – Abu Omar al-Baghdadi –
who may have led the organization until 2010.

However long Abu Bakr al-Baghdadi spent at Bucca
under the control of US troops, there is little doubt he
would have seen, heard of, and perhaps experienced
at least some of the brutality that characterized US
treatment of prisoners in Iraq. Only a few months before
al-Baghdadi was imprisoned at Bucca prison, the torture
photos from Abu Ghraib prison had been made public.
It is unclear whether any prisoners who experienced
that brutality at Abu Ghraib or elsewhere were present
at Bucca with al-Baghdadi, but it is certain that reports
of the torture were extensive throughout the US prison
system in Iraq.

The time in prison was also an opportunity for
strategic planning and recruiting for AQI's expanding
anti-occupation and anti-Shi'a resistance. Other former
prisoners in Bucca, in 2004 and later, recall al-Baghdadi's
arrival and the role he and others played in education,
organizing and planning for future military actions.
There is little doubt that al-Baghdadi's time in US
custody was instrumental in his rise to the leadership of
what would become one of the most powerful extremist
militias in the Middle East.

Before and during al-Baghdadi's incarceration in the US military prison, the anti-occupation resistance was rapidly expanding. As *The Guardian* described it, 'When Baghdadi, aged 33, arrived at Bucca, the Sunni-led anti-US insurgency was gathering steam across central and western Iraq. An invasion that had been sold as a war of liberation had become a grinding occupation. Iraq's Sunnis, disenfranchised by the overthrow of their patron, Saddam Hussein, were taking the fight to US forces – and starting to turn their guns towards the beneficiaries of Hussein's overthrow, the country's majority Shi'a population.'

Did the US troop surge in 2008 diminish sectarian fighting?

Although the Bush administration claimed that its troop 'surge' of 30,000 additional US military forces was the reason for the relative decline in sectarian fighting by 2008, the reality was far more complicated. It included the buying off of most of the leaders of Sunni tribal militias, the impact of a unilateral ceasefire declared in August 2007 by Shi'a militia leader Moqtada al-Sadr, and the horrific reality that the sectarian battles had largely achieved their goal. That is, by 2008 most mixed villages and towns had been ethnically cleansed to become almost entirely Sunni or Shi'a. Baghdad, historically a cosmopolitan mash-up of every religion and ethnicity, had become a city of districts defined by sect. Whether Sunni, Shi'a, Christian, or other, neighbourhoods were largely separated by giant cement blast walls.

In 2008, the US turned its commitment to paying the Sunni Awakening militias over to the Shi'a-dominated Iraqi government. Almost immediately, payments stopped, and the US-backed government under Prime Minister Nuri al-Maliki escalated its sectarian practices. More and more Sunni generals and other military leaders, as well as ordinary Sunni Iraqis, turned against the government even as US troops were slowly being withdrawn, and by 2009 and into 2010, a serious Sunni uprising was under way.

The Islamic State in Iraq, or ISI, had never joined the Sunni Awakening. It maintained its focus on fighting against the US occupation and the Iraqi government, although its military activities had diminished somewhat as the overall sectarian warfare had waned. But as the sectarian fighting escalated again in 2010, ISI re-emerged as a leading Sunni force, attacking the government, the official Iraqi military, and the expanding Shi'a militias allied to the government, as well as targeting Shi'a civilians. Abu Bakr al-Baghdadi was by that point (whether newly in power or not) the clear chief of ISI, and he began to strengthen the military capacity of the organization, including by several attacks on prisons aimed at freeing key military leaders of the group.

How did ISIS begin to expand beyond Iraq?

In 2011, ISI emerged for the first time across the border in Syria. The uprising there was just beginning to morph into a multifaceted civil war, and already the sectarian Sunni-Shi'a split was becoming a major component. That started with the proxy war between regional powers – Sunni Saudi Arabia and Shi'a Iran – but soon spilled over to include an internal divide between Syria's majority Sunni population and the minority but privileged Alawites, an offshoot of Shi'a Islam. ISI took up arms against the Alawite/Shi'a regime of Bashar al-Assad in Syria. ISI was fighting alongside the wide range of secular and Sunni militias – including the al-Qaeda-linked Jabhat an-Nusra, or Nusra Front – that were already confronting the regime. Soon, ISI turned to fight against those same anti-Assad forces, challenging those who rejected ISIS's power grabs, its violence, or its extremist definitions of Islam.

ISI changed its name again, this time to ISIS – for

the Islamic State in Iraq and Syria. By some accounts the acronym actually referred to the Islamic State in Iraq and al-Sham, Arabic for 'greater Syria'. (See 'How did the name ISIS evolve?') Still led by al-Baghdadi and loyal to al-Qaeda, ISIS was rapidly gaining strength, not least from its recruiting of experienced fighters and acquisition of heavier arms in Iraq. It fought on both sides of the Iraq-Syria frontier, against governments and civilians in both countries, capturing crossing posts and essentially erasing the border altogether. In Anbar province and other Sunni-majority parts of northern and central Iraq, ISIS was able to establish a large military presence, supported by many Sunnis as a useful protector against the Shi'a-dominated government's sectarian practices.

A major difference between ISIS and other militias, and particularly between ISIS and al-Qaeda, was that ISIS moved to seize territory. In doing so, it was not only asserting the theoretical goal of creating a future 'caliphate', it was actually doing so by occupying, holding, and governing an expanding land base across the Iraq-Syria border. In 2012 and into 2013, ISIS expanded its reach, establishing territorial control over large areas of northern Syria, including in and around the Syrian commercial centre of Aleppo. ISIS based its core governing functions in the city of Raqqa, which in mid-2014 was named its official capital.

Soon, however, relations deteriorated between ISIS and al-Qaeda, and between ISIS leader al-Baghdadi and al-Qaeda leader Ayman al-Zawahiri. From 2013 on, al-Baghdadi tried to bring the 'official' al-Qaeda Syrian franchise, the Nusra Front, under the control of ISIS. At one point ISIS announced that Nusra had 'merged' with ISIS, although Nusra denied the claim. Al-Qaeda leader al-Zawahiri, watching the rising power of ISIS and its ambitious leader, restated his official endorsement for the Nusra Front as al-Qaeda's official Syrian counterpart. There were other disagreements as well, including the divergence between al-Qaeda's religiously defined goal of establishing a global caliphate at some indeterminate point in the future and ISIS's tactic of seizing land, imposing its version of sharia law, and declaring it part of a present-day ISIS-run caliphate. The disagreements and power struggles continued, and in February 2014 al-Zawahiri officially renounced ISIS, criticizing, among other things, its violence against other Muslims.

Five months later, ISIS declared itself a global caliphate. Al-Baghdadi was named caliph, and once again the organization's name changed – this time to the 'Islamic State'. Since that time, small groups of Islamist militants in Sinai, Pakistan, Afghanistan and elsewhere have declared their loyalty to al-Baghdadi and the Islamic State, although it remains doubtful those links are operational. Throughout the summer of 2014, as the Iraqi military largely collapsed, ISIS moved aggressively to seize and consolidate its hold on large chunks of both Syria and Iraq, including Mosul, Iraq's second-largest city.

In August 2014 Patrick Cockburn wrote in the *London Review of Books*:

'The birth of the new state is the most radical change to the political geography of the Middle East since the Sykes-Picot Agreement was implemented in the aftermath of the First World War.'

As the militants continued to enlarge their territory and consolidate their control of an ever-expanding population across the two countries, the Obama administration renewed consideration of direct US military intervention against ISIS. By late summer 2014 at least 3,000 US troops were heading back into Iraq. And with the very real humanitarian crisis of Yazidi Syrians trapped on Mount Sinjar as a pretext, the US launched airstrikes against Syria.

America was officially at war with ISIS. As Peter Baker of the *New York Times* described it: 'In sending warplanes back into the skies over Iraq, President Obama... found himself exactly where he did not want to be. Hoping to end the war in Iraq, Mr Obama became the fourth president in a row to order military action in that graveyard of American ambition.'

Is there any precedent for the barbaric violence perpetrated by ISIS?

Much of what ISIS does is clear from massive international media coverage: kidnapping for ransom, whipping and other physical punishments, large-scale killing of civilians, and seizure of women and girls for rape and forced 'marriage' to fighters have all been well documented. Reports of ISIS destruction of irreplaceable, centuries-old works of art have devastated historians and archaeologists around the world. Some of the most shocking reported actions are used against those ISIS deems non-believers, including crucifixion and stoning to death. Some of those actions hark back to punishments used in ancient times. As is true of the eras in which the holy texts of other influential religions were written, the years of the Prophet Muhammad's life were also years of wars and constant battles for survival; that harsh wartime reality, including its punishments and its brutality, is reflected in the Qur'an as much as it is in the Torah, the Bible and other texts.

And yet some of these acts are also all too modern. Beheadings, for example, are currently used by governments, including the government of Saudi Arabia, as part of contemporary penal systems. Other actions, such as burning to death, also have contemporary forebears in the vigilante justice of mob actions, including the torture and burning to death of Christians in Pakistan or the 'necklacing' with burning tyres during the most difficult period of the South African liberation struggles. Perhaps no image is as powerful as these highly publicized killings – beheadings, particularly of Western journalists and aid workers, and the torture-death of Muath al-Kaseasbeh, a captured Jordanian bomber pilot, who was burned alive in a cage.

Those gruesome killings have come to symbolize the cruelty and violence at the core of ISIS, although it should be noted that these actions are hardly particular to the extremist organization. ISIS didn't invent the modern version of burning someone alive for revenge: Israeli extremists kidnapped a young Palestinian boy and burned him to death in June 2014, following the unrelated killing of three Israeli teenagers. Not too long ago, hundreds of mainly African-American men were burned to death – often after other horrifying tortures – in lynchings across the American South. That's aside from the even more common and more recent realities of burning people to death – civilians, children – with weapons of war designed to do just that, such as the napalm and white phosphorous used by the US in Vietnam and Iraq and by Israel in Gaza. There is also a long history of beheadings in world history; during the French Revolution the Jacobins are thought to have beheaded 17,000 people. Much more recently, in September 2014, the US-backed Free Syrian Army beheaded six ISIS captives, just days after ISIS beheaded two US journalists. And there is a longstanding legacy much closer to home, and much closer to ISIS: Saudi Arabia itself. In the first two weeks of 2015 alone, the government of Saudi Arabia beheaded 10 people for 'crimes' including apostasy, sorcery and witchcraft.

There are differences, of course. The Saudis arrested the journalist who leaked video of a recent beheading to the world; ISIS posts its carefully constructed videos on YouTube and other social media platforms to trumpet its crimes. The reason has much to do with ISIS's assumption that showing that level of violence, up close and personal, will also somehow demonstrate strength and commitment – and crucially, that it will show ISIS as winning. For some, there is also the attraction of violence itself. There are reports that some ISIS combatants and wannabe fighters, in particular international supporters, do not hold strong Islamic beliefs at all, but are actually attracted to the organization by the violence itself. Understanding that frightening reality is crucial to understanding how an organization so identified with violence can still gain support.

What are the motives and root causes underlying the ISIS tactic of public execution?

Each time ISIS kills a Western journalist or a Jordanian bomber pilot, the US, Jordan, Japan, or others, escalate their own direct military engagement. It was only after ISIS beheaded American journalists James Foley and Steven Sotloff in summer 2014 that the Obama administration finally announced it would send troops back to Iraq. It then returned to bombing Iraq and launched the first attacks in Syria. Japanese Prime Minister Shinzo Abe responded to the killing of Japanese journalist Kenji Goto with efforts to undermine Japan's longstanding pacifist constitution and promises to increase its engagement with the anti-ISIS war. Following the horrific killing of pilot Muath al-Kaseasbeh, the king of Jordan announced plans to increase its direct bombing raids against Syria and Iraq within the US 'coalition'.

As Stephen Kinzer wrote in the *Boston Globe* even before the killing of al-Kaseasbeh: 'By cleverly using grotesque theatrics, the Islamic State seems to be achieving its goal of luring the US back into war. It knows that the presence of American soldiers in the Middle East will attract more radicals and misguided idealists to its cause. For many of these young men and women, fighting Kurds or Shiite militias may not seem especially glorious. To face the mighty US on Middle Eastern soil, and if possible to kill an American or die at American hands, is their dream. We are giving them a chance to realize it. Through its impressive mastery of social media, the Islamic State is already using our escalation as a recruiting tool.'

What does ISIS believe?

It is not possible to generalize with any accuracy what individual ISIS fighters, supporters, or allies – reluctant or otherwise – think or believe. Many of those who support or even join ISIS appear to be motivated as much by diverse combinations of political, personal, or economic reasons as they are by adherence to any specific theological framework. For some, the humiliation of foreign occupation, the indignity of repressive rulers and the sense of disenfranchisement from one's own country play key motivating roles. We may never know exactly what each of those supporters believes. But the views of the leadership and the official positions of the organization are important for understanding who they are and why they act as they do – not to justify or apologize for its actions but precisely to figure out strategies that could actually work to stop its brutality, undermine its influence, and win its supporters away.

One way of defining what ISIS believes is to examine what distinguishes the group from its closest spiritual cousin and forebear, al-Qaeda, and the jihadi organizations still tied to al-Qaeda. Those distinctions include the nature of the 'caliphate' that al-Qaeda supports and ISIS has declared, the role and legitimacy of government, and – crucial to understand given the horrific brutality that characterizes ISIS – the role and purpose of violence.

When ISIS leader Abu Bakr al-Baghdadi declared himself the caliph, or leader, of his just-announced Islamic state, or caliphate, in June 2014, he was claiming a direct linkage to a much older religious/political position of power. The last caliphate was dissolved by the newly secular Turkish Republic in 1924 following the defeat of the Ottoman Empire in World War I.

Like earlier Islamist organizations, including al-Qaeda, ISIS had already been advocating the idea of rebuilding the original caliphate, a term for the territory ruled by an Islamic leader, which came into use following the death of the Prophet Muhammad. But, unlike al-Qaeda, ISIS actually went ahead and acted to create a caliphate. The Islamic State declared by ISIS would be built in an undefined swath of the Arab world and perhaps beyond, beginning with the territory ISIS already controlled across Syria and Iraq. But its call for all Muslims and Islamist organizations to pledge fealty to al-Baghdadi as the new caliph was seen as a direct challenge, especially to al-Qaeda, which had already been feuding with ISIS over both political and religious differences.

A major point of divergence was precisely on the question of whether the caliphate could be declared now, today, as ISIS claimed, or whether it was a goal to be sought in the future, as al-Qaeda's leaders had long asserted. Part of that question has to do with whether the legitimacy of a caliphate requires its collective approval by Muslim scholars, or even the *umma*, or Muslim community as a whole, or whether an individual Muslim leader can simply proclaim a caliphate as his own.

As the *New York Times*' David Kirkpatrick described the two sides: 'Al-Qaeda's ideologues have been more vehement. All insist that the promised caliphate requires a broad consensus, on behalf of Muslim scholars if not all Muslims, and not merely one man's proclamation after a military victory. "Will this caliphate be a sanctuary for all the oppressed and a refuge for every Muslim?" Abu Muhammad al-Maqdisi, a senior jihadist scholar, recently asked in a statement on the internet. "Or will this creation take a sword against all the Muslims who oppose it" and "nullify all the groups that do jihad in the name of God?"'

Another point of disagreement between al-Qaeda and ISIS has to do with government. When the original caliphate, which held both religious and governing power, was dismantled in 1924, the Muslim Brotherhood in Egypt was the first Islamist organization to emerge in that new period. Its goal was to contend for political power with the new secular forces rising in the Islamic world.

The Muslim Brotherhood became the model for generations of Islamist organizations that followed, engaging in political struggles – sometimes armed, often not – to win political power. But supporters of the most literal Wahhabi traditions refused to support any secular government; they recognized only the caliphate itself as holding legitimate power. All others, anyone who supported a secular or even religious government, would be considered a traitor, often sentenced to death. This shapes the antagonism of ISIS to organizations like today's Muslim Brotherhood in Egypt, the democratic Islamist Ennahda Party in Tunisia, Hamas in Palestine, and others, and it forms much of the basis of the split between ISIS and al-Qaeda itself.

Al-Qaeda, of course, never attempted to govern on its own. Its goals had to do with overthrowing governments, particularly the Saudi monarchy, which it deemed insufficiently pious and too corrupt to be worthy of support. But it didn't try to create a replacement government. When al-Qaeda took refuge in Afghanistan in the 1990s, it did nothing to challenge the Taliban government, nor to attempt any efforts to rule anywhere in the country.

But ISIS – having swept through and captured huge swaths of territory in both Iraq and Syria, including large cities with a population estimated at five to six million people – now has to figure out how to govern in the modern world. However medieval its ideology, this urgency explains the group's efforts to recruit doctors, engineers, teachers and other professionals, and to bribe and threaten local experts into remaining on the job. ISIS officials need to find people able to keep the electricity on and the water clean and flowing, to keep hospitals open and medicine accessible. That means money, which means increasing efforts to sell oil, mostly though not entirely on the black market, from oil-producing areas under its control, and to raise other funds through taxes on businesses under its authority, along with extortion and kidnappings for ransom.

Al-Qaeda could concentrate on carrying out acts of violence aimed at destroying ungodly governments; ISIS needs to govern. And it may be that over time, the inability to provide ordinary people caught in ISIS-controlled territory with the ordinary requirements of life – jobs, electricity, schools, water, food, doctors – may lead to its collapse.

Finally there is a significant divide regarding the use of violence. It's not quite accurate to claim, as many in the media did, that al-Qaeda broke with ISIS because it was 'too violent'. The conflict is less over the amount or nature of the violence than it is about the purpose and the chosen victims. The essential al-Qaeda critique, in a sense, is not that ISIS was 'too violent' but that it used violence for the wrong reasons against too many Muslims.

For al-Qaeda, violence was primarily understood as necessary to overthrow heretical, or insufficiently devout governments – starting with Saudi Arabia because the monarchy there has power over the holiest shrines of Islam – and those governments that keep them in power, most notably the US. ISIS looked back to an earlier tradition. Princeton scholar Bernard Haykel describes ISIS as relying on 'a kind of untamed Wahhabism' that saw violence as having a much more privileged position.

As the *New York Times* describes it, 'al-Qaeda grew out of a radical tradition that viewed Muslim states and societies as having fallen into sinful unbelief, and embraced violence as a tool to redeem them. But the Wahhabi tradition embraced the killing of those deemed unbelievers as essential to purifying the community of the faithful.' That is the ISIS approach. Haykel described how 'violence is part of their ideology. For al-Qaeda, violence is a means to an end; for ISIS, it is an end in itself.'

Another aspect of the ISIS belief system has to do

with an apocalyptic vision of the end time, which they believe is coming very soon. The ISIS countdown to Armageddon is shaped by a Manichean notion (based on some early Islamic theology) of a battle between Muslims and crusaders. In its particular version, ISIS will lead the Muslims to victory in or near the small Syrian town of Dabiq, near the Turkish border, which ISIS occupied in the summer of 2014.

As Graeme Wood described in his widely read *Atlantic* article examining the group's theology and beliefs: 'ISIS has attached great importance to the Syrian city of Dabiq, near Aleppo. It named its propaganda magazine after the town, and celebrated madly when (at great cost) it conquered Dabiq's strategically unimportant plains. It is here, the Prophet reportedly said, that the armies of Rome will set up their camp. The armies of Islam will meet them, and Dabiq will be Rome's Waterloo or its Antietam... The [ISIS] magazine quotes Zarqawi as saying, "The spark has been lit here in Iraq, and its heat will continue to intensify... until it burns the crusader armies in Dabiq."'

There is historical significance to Dabiq. In 1516 the town was the site of a major defeat of the Mamluk Sultan by the early Ottomans. But, for ISIS, what is most important is the belief that Islam – in this case ISIS itself – will defeat the armies of Rome, or the crusaders, in Dabiq. For the ISIS leadership, the importance of conquering this militarily insignificant town seems to have been based on the idea that ISIS can wait there for the arrival of an enemy army which it will then conquer.

The willingness of ISIS to wait for the crusader army to show up explains a great deal about the goal of its most gruesome atrocities. ISIS wants to provoke an attack by its enemies – the US, the West, the crusaders – on its own turf, just as the Qur'an predicts. The ISIS propaganda strategy is based on the understanding that the odds of Western armies coming across the world to attack ISIS in its own territory rise dramatically if ISIS can outrage Western public opinion. And the strategy has worked. The US and its allies decided to attack ISIS directly, rather than through proxies, only after public outrage at the horrors of ISIS treatment of prisoners and captured civilians.

In sending US planes to bomb ISIS in Syria and US troops and special forces to fight against ISIS in Iraq, in supporting US allies like Saudi Arabia, Turkey, Jordan, and the UAE to attack ISIS throughout the region, the US and its allies are giving ISIS exactly what it wants.

What is Wahhabism? Why is it relevant to understanding ISIS?

For the leaders of ISIS, and despite the intensity of official Saudi opposition to it, the group's roots lie directly in the Wahhabi branch of Sunni Islam, which officially governs Saudi Arabia.

At its core and in its practice, ISIS is a thoroughly modern organization, but understanding it involves going back to the 18th century, when the Muslim caliphate within the Ottoman Empire was losing territory and power. As the renowned scholar of religion Karen Armstrong noted in the *New Statesman*, this occurred in the same period when Europe was just beginning to separate church and state – a new phenomenon tied to modernism and the Enlightenment. The Muslim leadership of the caliphate did not believe in such a divide, and instead a variety of reformist movements emerged, whose followers believed that 'if Muslims were to regain lost power and prestige, they must return to the fundamentals of their faith, ensuring that God – rather than materialism or worldly ambition – dominated the political order. There was nothing militant about this "fundamentalism"; rather, it was a grassroots attempt to reorient society and did not involve jihad.'

One of those movements was led by a scholar from central Arabia named Muhammad Ibn Abd al-Wahhab.

Many local leaders rejected his approach, but he found a patron in a powerful local tribal leader, Muhammad Ibn Saud. In the local wars rising among the largely nomadic desert tribes for goods and land, Saud used Wahhabism to justify its opposite: his military campaigns were clearly fought for political and economic power. As Armstrong describes it, 'two forms of Wahhabism were emerging: where Ibn Saud was happy to enforce Wahhabi Islam with the sword to enhance his political position, Ibn Abd al-Wahhab insisted that education, study, and debate were the only legitimate means of spreading the one true faith.'

When Wahhab died, Saud and later his sons continued to claim that Wahhabism was the only legitimate version of Islam and that it could be 'enforced with the sword'. Enforcing the Wahhabi version of Islam along with the practice of *takfir*, meaning identifying other Muslims as unbelievers and therefore deserving of death, became common ways of justifying mass killings that actually were committed for political or economic goals. Armstrong describes how, after Wahhab's death, 'Wahhabism became more violent, an instrument of state terror... Saud's son and successor used *takfir* to justify the wholesale slaughter of resistant populations. In 1801, his army sacked the holy Shia city of Karbala in what is now Iraq, plundered the tomb of Imam Husain, and slaughtered thousands of Shias, including women and children; in 1803, in fear and panic, the holy city of Mecca surrendered to the Saudi leader.'

That was the origin of what would later – following World War I and British and French colonial machinations – become the state of Saudi Arabia. During the decades that followed, competing violent strands of Wahhabism vied for power and influence, including a rebel movement known as the Ikhwan, or brotherhood. With the quashing of the Ikhwan rebellion in 1930, the replacement of its rejection of modernity, and its extreme violence against civilians who disagreed with it, the official Saudi state presented a changed version of Wahhabism. Saudi Arabia abandoned the majority of the most violent practices, including the territorial expansion efforts that lay at the heart of early Wahhabism.

Unsurprisingly, not everyone agreed with that shift. There were struggles over the definitions, goals and traditions of Wahhabi Islam, and in many ways ISIS now shows its roots in some of those earlier practices. As Karen Armstrong describes the trajectory, 'the Ikhwan spirit and its dream of territorial expansion did not die, but gained new ground in the 1970s, when the kingdom became central to Western foreign policy in the region. Washington welcomed the Saudis' opposition to Nasserism (the pan-Arab socialist ideology of Egypt's second president, Gamal Abdel Nasser) and to Soviet influence. After the Iranian Revolution, it [Washington] gave tacit support to the Saudis' project of countering Shia radicalism by Wahhabizing the entire Muslim world... Like the Ikhwan, IS represents a rebellion against the official Wahhabism of modern Saudi Arabia. Its swords, covered faces and cut-throat executions all recall the original Brotherhood.'

Of course the immediate political trajectory of ISIS as an organization lies in the much more recent past, specifically the years of US occupation of Iraq and the rise of al-Qaeda. But its religious and ideological touchstones have much older roots, in Saudi Arabia, not Iraq.

How did the name ISIS evolve?

The organization known as ISIS, or the Islamic State in Iraq and Syria (or for some, the Islamic State in Iraq and al-Sham), traces its origins to the earlier ISI, or Islamic State in Iraq, which was itself an outgrowth of al-Qaeda in Iraq (AQI), sometimes known as al-Qaeda in Mesopotamia. Beginning in June 2014, ISIS changed its name again and began to refer to itself as the Islamic State, or IS. The organization has also been known as ISIL, or the Islamic State in Iraq and the Levant. In much of the Arab world, it is known as Daesh, the Arabic acronym for al-Dawla al-Islamiya fil-Iraq wash-Sham (more or less the same as ISIS).

The original name, al-Qaeda in Iraq, reflected the origins of the group, claiming the Iraqi franchise of the al-Qaeda brand. The name change from al-Qaeda in Iraq, or AQI, to Islamic State of Iraq, or ISI, took place during the US troop surge in 2006-07, when many Sunni militias were abandoning their opposition to the US occupation and instead joining the US-initiated Awakening movement, which paid them to fight with the US occupation forces instead of against them. The newly renamed ISI, which rejected the Awakening movement and continued its anti-occupation military attacks, was thus distinguishing itself from its former allies among other Sunni militias.

The next change, to ISIS or the Islamic State in Iraq and Syria, came when the organization, after the 2009-10 period of not-quite-defeat but certainly significant setbacks in Iraq, re-emerged in Syria as a rising player on the anti-Assad side of the Syrian civil war. This change also heralded the more ambitious self-definition of the group's intentions – beyond the geographic expansion from Iraq to Syria, it was also now looking toward the elimination of the Syrian-Iraqi border as part of its goal. ISIS, whether one defines the final 'S' as Syria or al-Sham, refers to an older, pre-colonial definition of the territory: what was long known as 'Greater Syria',

Al-Sham, Arabic for Greater Syria, referred to a wide and diverse territory that had been under control of the Ottoman Empire for 400 or so years. It included more or less today's Syria, Lebanon, Jordan, and historic Palestine, including what is now Israel. So 'ISIS' generally refers both to the location of the group's fighters and supporters – contemporary Iraq and Syria – and the aspirations of the organization. ISIS has been public about its goal of erasing colonial borders, starting with the border between Iraq and Syria, but it is easy to see its goals extending to reversing the colonially imposed divide between Syria and Lebanon and beyond. ISIS has said little about the issue of Palestine, but it's difficult to imagine any discussion of colonial borders in the Middle East that did not quickly turn to Israel-Palestine.

The alternative contemporary version of the name, ISIL, or Islamic State in Iraq and the Levant, may have emerged as a consequence of translation, rather than as the organization's own choice. The group itself uses 'al-Sham' in its names, thus ISIS in translation. But al-Sham, historically, was the same thing as the Levant, a European term both colonialist and orientalist in its origins and usage. So the Obama administration's conscious choice to use 'ISIL' rather than 'ISIS' reflects a deliberate intention to be insulting.

As Public Radio International's 'The World' programme explains it, 'The term Levant first appeared in medieval French. It literally means "the rising", referring to the land where the sun rises. If you're in France, in the western Mediterranean, that would make sense as a way to describe the eastern Mediterranean.' Thus the colonialist legacy. PRI goes on, 'Levant was also used in English from at least 1497. It's kind of archaic, but still used by scholars in English, though more widely in French. The Germans have a similar term for the same region: *Morgenland*, or "the land of the morning", It's even more archaic in German and kind of implies an imaginary, romantic, never-never land.' Thus the orientalist part.

Even the *New York Times* identified 'Levant' as 'a once-common term that now has something of an antique whiff about it, like "the Orient", Because of the term's French colonial associations, many Arab nationalists and Islamist radicals disdain it, and it is unlikely that the militant group would choose "Levant" to render its name.' But for the White House, apparently colonialist language does not seem to present a problem. At least through the spring of 2015, ISIL remained the

Obama administration's chosen term. There has been significant media attention paid to the word choice, but no clarity from the White House itself.

Among Arabic speakers, the most common choice is the acronym Daesh, or Da'ish, essentially the Arabic version of ISIS, but with quite negative overtones. *The Guardian* notes that 'in Arabic, the word lends itself to being snarled with aggression. As Simon Collis, the British ambassador to Iraq, told *The Guardian*'s Ian Black: "Arabic speakers spit out the name Da'ish with different mixtures of contempt, ridicule and hostility. Da'ish is always negative."'

Not surprisingly, some news outlets, governments, analysts and others have been reluctant to use the term 'Islamic State' to describe the militants seeking power across large parts of Iraq and Syria. They believe that using the term would give credibility to the violent extremist organization's claim that it is a real state, a caliphate or Islamic state that somehow has authority over the world's Muslims or at least is deserving of recognition as a state. For those who do use the term, the reasoning seems to be grounded primarily in pragmatic considerations: if this is the title the organization has given itself, we'll use it for now, but using it doesn't imply any endorsement.

But the term 'Islamic State', or IS, without the geographic specificity of the earlier ISI and ISIS versions, does have a propaganda purpose. The organization's name change was not arbitrary; indeed it was announced in the context of the declaration of a caliphate – not as a religious vision for end times but in today's real world, in real territory, in which it is governing real cities populated by real people. National Public Radio quoted a former Senate Foreign Relations Committee staff analyst who described the name change to Islamic State as 'a very potent area of propaganda, because ISIS has attracted potentially thousands of foreign fighters, and none of these foreign fighters see themselves as terrorists. They see themselves as knights. They see themselves as *mujahideen*. They see themselves as freedom fighters...So they're very interested in fighting for the Islamic State.'

Over time the brutality of ISIS rule and its inability to provide for the basic needs of the populations it controls will certainly undermine its support. But in the meantime, the claim of creating a whole new society, an Islamic State, however brutal it may be, has played a major role in encouraging the large-scale recruitment to ISIS-controlled territory not only of fighters but also of doctors, engineers, computer nerds, indeed whole families from around the world.

Did ISIS emerge because Obama pulled troops out of Iraq?

Many political opponents of the Obama administration, including (though not limited to) supporters of even more robust US military action in the Middle East, claim that the seemingly sudden emergence of ISIS was the direct result of the pullout of US troops from Iraq. This notion gained traction because of the timing of the two events. ISIS's powerful military sweep across northern Syria and then into Iraq began just over a year after the last US troops left Iraq in December 2011. But the troop withdrawal was not the reason for the rise of ISIS in either Iraq or Syria.

ISIS's re-emergence in Iraq after a period of relative quiescence in 2009-10 came in response to the escalating anti-Sunni sectarianism of the Shi'a-dominated government in Baghdad that was still armed, paid and supported by the US even while troop numbers were being reduced.

Before that, the origins and influence of ISIS in Iraq lie in the invasion and occupation of that country, which began in 2003 under George W Bush, not in the 2011 withdrawal of US troops. ISIS emerged in Iraq in 2004, as one of numerous Sunni militias fighting against the US, British and other coalition forces and later against the so-called Iraqi Interim Government.

As the anti-occupation war became increasingly sectarian, the Sunni AQI/ISIS continued to clash with the Shi'a-dominated, US-backed Iraqi government.

In 2006 and 2007, the Bush administration sent thousands of additional troops during the so-called surge in Iraq and organized the Sunni Awakening movement. ISIS had not joined the Awakening movement, but it was significantly weakened in the 2007-08 period, when it lost support of Sunni communities and tribes, many of which were taking money from the Awakening movement and pulling back from the military struggle. When the US turned over responsibility for paying the Sunni tribes to the Shi'a-dominated – and increasingly sectarian – Iraqi government, the government of Prime Minister Nuri al-Maliki stopped payments and escalated attacks against Sunni communities. Inevitably, the sectarian tensions increased and set the stage for the emergence of what amounted to a Sunni revolt against the government and an increase in Sunni support for ISIS.

Large-scale fighting started again by early 2009, and ISIS re-emerged as a major force, this time within the renewed Sunni uprising. Its target was primarily the Shi'a government, which had already signed an agreement with the Bush administration requiring the withdrawal of all US troops and all Pentagon-paid military contractors from Iraq by the end of 2011.

The new Obama administration actually reopened the withdrawal plan, trying to convince Iraq to allow up to 20,000 US troops to remain, but the negotiations foundered over the question of impunity. Prime Minister al-Maliki was reportedly in favour of keeping US troops in Iraq beyond the deadlines. But Iraq refused to grant Washington's demand that US troops be assured of absolute immunity for any war crimes they might commit, and without that impunity, presumably knowing that US troops would certainly continue to commit war crimes, the US refused to keep any troops in Iraq.

The repression by the Shi'a-dominated Iraqi government increased, the Sunni uprising escalated, and full-scale sectarian war resumed, with US participation through the end of 2011 and without the US starting in 2012. War continued, and ISIS played a major role in the sectarian battle. Under US pressure, in August 2014 al-Maliki was replaced by another politician from the same Shi'a party.

New prime minister Haider al-Abadi talked a more inclusive line, including announcing that his government would stop bombing Sunni communities, but he did little to change the sectarian practices of the military and police agencies, and thus the sectarian pressures continued. Sunni former generals, Sunni tribal leaders and others continued to resist the repression. Many of them continued their alliance with ISIS, seeing it as the strongest opposition to the US-backed government. Using a combination of conventional military tactics and the brutality it had become known for, including kidnappings, beheadings and sex slavery, ISIS fought against both Iraqi government forces and civilians: Shi'a, Christians, Yazidis, even Sunnis who did not accept its extremist interpretation of Islam. The Sunni revolt continued even as ISIS moved to consolidate its seizure of land and expansion into Syria, which would define the regional war for years to come.

Whatever the beliefs and intentions of ISIS leadership, its revival and renewed Sunni support – which made possible its rapid success within the Sunni revolt in Iraq – were directly linked to the continuing sectarian marginalization and repression against Sunnis by the US-backed and Shi'a-dominated government in Baghdad. So the origins and rise of ISIS stem from the US invasion and occupation of Iraq, not the belated withdrawal of US troops.

Where does ISIS get its money from?

Along with selling oil it produces from oilfields and refineries in territories it has seized, ISIS relies on several other sources of funding, including taxes levied on businesses within, and transporting of goods in and out of, cities, towns, and areas under its control. As ISIS consolidated its governance in northern Syria and western Iraq after declaring itself the Islamic State 'caliphate' in 2014, it began to operate as if it were an actual government. While some of this was purely for appearances, ISIS did begin to issue commercial, building, and drivers' licences to carry out at least the basics of running public utilities, the operation of schools and medical facilities, and to collect taxes.

Taxes took the form of official-sounding taxes that any government might assess for commercial or other actions, as well as straight-up extortion. That reportedly included ISIS skimming money off the top of salary funds the Iraqi government is still paying to civil service workers in ISIS-occupied Mosul. Since ISIS took control of the central bank in Mosul, the salaries of government workers have been paid in cash picked up weekly by emissaries from the occupied city who meet directly with Iraqi government officials outside of Mosul.

ISIS has also gained hundreds of thousands, if not millions, as ransom from the families, businesses or governments of its kidnapping victims. While the US and Britain maintain staunch 'no payment of ransom' positions and have seen numerous US and British nationals killed by ISIS (as well as by other extremist organizations), various European, Asian, and other countries – both governments and companies – have brought their people home after quietly paying ransoms generally far lower than those demanded for American or British citizens.

Then there is the massive funding, by some reports second only to oil income, accruing to ISIS from sales of plundered ancient artifacts, putting the historical legacy of Syria and to some degree Iraq at even greater risk. The human rights section of the American Association for the Advancement of Science took satellite images in 2014 that, according to a scholar on the project, 'show the destruction of ancient artifacts, architecture, and most importantly, archaeological context that is the record of humanity's past. From the origins of civilization to the first international empires, Syria's cultural heritage and these sites in particular are vitally important to our understanding of history.' Some of those looted artifacts are being sold to collectors and dealers in the US. According to a February 2015 *Wall Street Journal* investigation, 'in the US alone, government data show the value of declared antiques imported from Syria jumped 134 per cent in 2013 to $11 million. US officials estimate the value of undeclared pieces is many multiples higher.'

And ISIS is not the only force threatening Syria's cultural treasure. The *Journal* article reports that 'video published by a Syrian opposition media network on YouTube shows soldiers fighting for President Bashar al-Assad 's regime at Palmyra with delicate grave reliefs loaded onto a truck. And senior Free Syrian Army fighters, the secular opposition that has received aid from the US, have long conceded to Western media that looting antiquities is an important source of funding.'

In early 2015, the United Nations Security Council passed a series of resolutions aimed at choking off sources of funding for ISIS as well as other extremist organizations including the al-Nusra Front. The Council condemned the purchase of oil from those organizations. But although it passed the resolution under Chapter VII of the UN Charter, which can authorize the use of force, it did little to bring real pressure on the global oil market to stop the trade, threatening only to send any violators to the UN Sanctions Committee for possible listing as a violator of UN sanctions. It called on all UN member states to freeze the assets of people who commit terrorist acts, and to 'take appropriate steps to prevent the trade in Iraqi and Syrian cultural property and other items of... historical, cultural, rare scientific and religious importance illegally removed from Iraq since 6 August 1990 [when the first resolution aimed at protecting Iraqi cultural heritage was passed] and from Syria since 15 March 2011.' The resolution also reaffirmed that payment of ransom to any organization on the UN's al-Qaeda sanctions list, regardless of who pays, would be considered a violation of international legal obligations.

Then there is the politically embarrassing (for the US, at least) source of some of the most crucial funding for ISIS – important because it provides political and military as well as direct financial support. That source is the US-backed, US-armed petro-monarchies of the Arab Gulf: Saudi Arabia, Kuwait, the UAE, Qatar and beyond.

Writing in *CounterPunch* in February 2015, Patrick Cockburn reported that ISIS

is still receiving significant financial support from Arab sympathizers outside Iraq and Syria, enabling it to expand its war effort, says a senior Kurdish official. The US has been trying to stop such private donors in the Gulf oil states sending to Islamic State (ISIS) funds that help pay the salaries of fighters who may number well over 100,000. Fuad Hussein, the chief of staff of the Kurdish President, Massoud Barzani, told *The Independent on Sunday*: 'There is sympathy for Da'esh [ISIS] in many Arab countries and this has translated into money – and that is a disaster.' ... Dr Mahmoud Othman, a veteran member of the Iraqi Kurdish leadership who recently retired from the Iraqi parliament, said there was a misunderstanding as to why Gulf countries paid off IS. It is not only that donors are supporters of IS, but that the movement 'gets money from the Arab countries because they are afraid of it,' he says. 'Gulf countries give money to Da'esh so that it promises not to carry out operations on their territory.'

Some of the most extensive reports are of direct

funding of ISIS (as well as of the plethora of extreme Islamist organizations that preceded it) by Saudi Arabia, though the exact combination of government funds, state-linked institutional funds, donations from individual princes within the vast royal family, and contributions from wealthy individuals and businesses in the kingdom remains murky. This isn't a new, or an ISIS-specific phenomenon. As Patrick Cockburn notes in his book *The Jihadis Return*:

> In 2009, eight years after 9/11, a cable from the US Secretary of State, Hillary Clinton, revealed by WikiLeaks, complained that donors in Saudi Arabia constituted the most significant source of funding to Sunni terrorist groups worldwide. But despite this private admission, the US and Western Europeans continued to remain indifferent to Saudi preachers whose message, spread to millions by satellite TV, YouTube and Twitter, called for the killing of the Shi'a as heretics. These calls came as al-Qaeda bombs were slaughtering people in Shi'a neighborhoods in Iraq. A sub-headline in another State Department cable in the same year reads: 'Saudi Arabia: Anti-Shi'ism As Foreign Policy?' Now, five years later, Saudi-supported groups have a record of extreme sectarianism against non-Sunni Muslims.'

The US knew, but despite it all, the Saudi monarchy – known for its tight control over its own population – remained a key Washington ally.

There was of course a long history of Saudi funding of Islamic extremists in official and unacknowledged partnerships with the US. During the 1980s it was Saudi money that paid for the Afghan *mujahideen* warriors, trained and backed by the CIA and Pakistan's ISI intelligence services, who battled Soviet-backed forces at Washington's behest at the height of Reagan's Cold War. There are countless reports of Saudi involvement in the 9/11 attacks themselves, in which 15 of the 19 hijackers were Saudi citizens; the storied 28-page section of the official 9/11 report, which remains fully redacted and unavailable to the public, allegedly details some of that involvement. The focus on that potential scandal had waned in recent years. But it gained new prominence with the sudden announcement in February 2015 that al-Qaeda operative and so-called 20th hijacker Zacarias Moussaoui, serving a life sentence in a US prison, had testified in a related trial about the powerful Saudi princes who had funded bin Laden's and others' terrorist actions. He named names, including Prince Turki al-Faisal, the former Saudi intelligence chief; Prince Bandar bin Sultan, Saudi ambassador to the US; influential billionaire Prince al-Waleed bin Talal; and many of Saudi Arabia's most powerful clerics. All the princes (though probably not the imams) had long experience in and with the US, some in close relationships at the highest levels of US government.

Other regional leaders have been even more direct in holding the Gulf monarchies responsible for the rise in extremism. US-backed Iraqi President Nuri al-Maliki, in March 2014, blamed Saudi Arabia and Qatar. As quoted by Patrick Cockburn in *The Jihadis Return*, Maliki told an interviewer that 'these two countries are primarily responsible for the sectarian, terrorist and security crisis in Iraq.' While part of his goal was to deflect his government's own responsibility for its sectarian, anti-Sunni repression, Maliki went on to say that the two governments were also 'buying weapons for the benefit of these terrorist organizations.' According to Cockburn, 'there was considerable truth in Maliki's charges.'

Such allegations are consistent with longstanding and now public US government unease over funding of terrorists coming from the Gulf states allied to the US. When *The Guardian* and other outlets were releasing the huge trove of WikiLeaks cables in 2009-10, one set dealt directly with US concerns about Saudi and other Gulf states' funding of Islamist extremists, in the years when

ISIS was still functioning as al-Qaeda in Iraq and as the Islamic State of Iraq.

According to *The Guardian*:

> Saudi Arabia is the world's largest source of funds for Islamist militant groups such as the Afghan Taliban and Lashkar-e-Taiba – but the Saudi government is reluctant to stem the flow of money, according to Hillary Clinton. 'More needs to be done since Saudi Arabia remains a critical financial support base for al-Qaeda, the Taliban, LeT [the Pakistani terrorist group Lashkar-e-Taiba, responsible for the deadly Mumbai attack of 2008] and other terrorist groups,' says a secret December 2009 paper signed by the US secretary of state.
>
> 'Donors in Saudi Arabia constitute the most significant source of funding to Sunni terrorist groups worldwide,' she said. Three other Arab countries are listed as sources of militant money: Qatar, Kuwait and the United Arab Emirates... Saudi officials are often painted as reluctant partners. Clinton complained of the 'ongoing challenge to persuade Saudi officials to treat terrorist funds emanating from Saudi Arabia as a strategic priority'...
>
> In common with its neighbours, Kuwait is described as a 'source of funds and a key transit point' for al-Qaeda and other militant groups. While the government has acted against attacks on its own soil, it is 'less inclined to take action against Kuwait-based financiers and facilitators plotting attacks outside of Kuwait'.

Saudi funding, whether from individuals, government-backed institutions, or Saudi princes themselves, would certainly fit with the religious/political support for Sunni Islamist extremism that has characterized Saudi domestic and foreign policy for decades. That policy has included a powerful anti-Shi'a component that fits easily with lethal treatment by ISIS of Shi'a in the areas it controls. Storied Middle East correspondent Robert Fisk wrote in July 2014 that:

Some time before 9/11, Prince Bandar bin Sultan, once the powerful Saudi ambassador in Washington and head of Saudi intelligence until a few months ago, had a revealing and ominous conversation with the head of the British Secret Intelligence Service, MI6, Sir Richard Dearlove. Prince Bandar told him: 'The time is not far off in the Middle East, Richard, when it will be literally "God help the Shi'a". More than a billion Sunnis have simply had enough of them.'

The fatal moment predicted by Prince Bandar may now have come for many Shi'a, with Saudi Arabia playing an important role in bringing it about by supporting the anti-Shi'a jihad in Iraq and Syria...

Dearlove, who headed MI6 from 1999 to 2004, emphasized the significance of Prince Bandar's words, saying that they constituted 'a chilling comment that I remember very well indeed.' He does not doubt that substantial and sustained funding from private donors in Saudi Arabia and Qatar, to which the authorities may have turned a blind eye, has played a central role in the Isis surge into Sunni areas of Iraq. He said: 'Such things simply do not happen spontaneously'...

Dearlove's explosive revelation about the prediction of a day of reckoning for the Shi'a by Prince Bandar, and the former head of MI6's view that Saudi Arabia is involved in the ISIS-led Sunni rebellion, has attracted surprisingly little attention.

Perhaps that refusal to pay attention is not so surprising, particularly in Washington. For much of that time, the US not only relied on Saudi Arabia as one of its most important Middle East strategic partners, but also sold tens of billions of dollars' worth of the most sophisticated US weapons. In return, of course, the Saudis guaranteed the US access to and significant levels of influence on their enormous oil-production process.

How does ISIS treat women and what is the role of women within the organization?

Islamic fundamentalists, as is the case with most of their

counterparts in other religions, do not believe women are equal to men. From ISIS to al-Qaeda, from the Taliban to the government of Saudi Arabia, women are deemed not only different from men but lesser. Although some parts of Islamic law provide (at least aspirationally) some level of social protections for women, including economic security, in the real world women have little access to basic human rights. Women are excluded from much of public life, with severe restrictions on whether and in what jobs they can work. Many basic aspects of women's lives, including decisions regarding their children, access to healthcare and education, legal status, and passports, remain under the control of their husbands, fathers, sons, or other male relatives.

In areas under ISIS control, women live under an extreme version of these restrictions. Aside from the limitations on their daily lives, the reports of what ISIS does to women in areas it captures are truly horrifying. Women kidnapped, raped, murdered, sold as slaves to fighters: the list goes on. Women are often taken and held as sex slaves or other roles when the men in a captured village or town are killed on the spot. The women targeted for such crimes are often non-Sunnis – Shi'a or Yazidi or Christian perhaps – but in some cases they may also include Sunnis who do not accept the extremist definitions of religion demanded by ISIS. In November 2014 CBS News reported an assault on a Sunni tribe in Iraq, in Ras al-Maa, a village near Ramadi, the capital of Anbar Province, now largely controlled by ISIS. In that attack, a senior member of the local Sunni al-Bu Nimr tribe described how at least 50 people were lined up and shot, one by one, of whom four were children and six were women.

So the punishments unique to women – including rape and forced 'marriage' to ISIS fighters – are carried out even as women suffer the non-gender-specific attacks alongside men. Women, indeed whole families, become victims of kidnappings, are forced from their homes, and face the risks inherent in US and coalition air strikes and other attacks aimed at ISIS.

Unfortunately many of the atrocities committed specifically against women are more quantitatively than qualitatively different from misogynistic traditions still in practice in some areas where ISIS has established a base and elsewhere. Forced marriage, for example, including the marriage of young girls, is a widespread phenomenon in poor rural areas of several Arab, African, and Asian countries.

The period of Taliban rule in Afghanistan, and its overthrow in the US invasion and occupation that began in October 2001, provides a useful model. Treatment of women under Taliban rule was abysmal: many schools shut down, girls forced to leave school, urban women forced out of many professions, violently enforced restrictions on women's actions, autonomy, dress, and more. Many girls and women were forced into marriages against their will. The US justified much of its anti-Taliban military engagement in Afghanistan with the language of protecting Afghan women. But it turned out that many of the warlords who had fought and lost to the Taliban, and later came back to fight with the US against the Taliban, held medieval-era views of women's role in society that were strikingly similar to those of the Taliban.

When the US imposed a modern, more or less gender-equality-based constitution and laws, life improved for a small sector of Afghan women – those in Kabul and the few other large cities. But for the majority of women in the country, things did not get better. Forced marriages were a longstanding custom in many regions of rural Afghanistan (where the vast majority of the population lived), and they did not disappear when the US and its chosen proxies overthrew the Taliban. In fact, anti-Taliban warlords known for committing atrocities at times ended up in powerful positions in post-Taliban Afghanistan, including in the US-backed government.

Aside from the direct attacks on women, ISIS

restrictions on women in public life are severe, including limits on schooling, separation of the sexes, prohibitions on many areas of work. There is no question the actions of ISIS are brutal and misogynistic. But it is also true that with the announcement of the Islamic State as a 'caliphate', ISIS asserted the goal of building a fully Islamic society, requiring the involvement of whole families, including women and children.

That state-building project is one of the key distinctions between ISIS and other extremist Islamist organizations. *Time* magazine's Vivienne Walt described how

> in al-Qaeda's wars in Afghanistan and Iraq, young armed men holed up on the battlefield far from their families. But in Syria ISIS aims to install a purist Islamic state – an entire new country – as its name denotes. And so ISIS fighters are looking to build lives that are far broader than fighting the war, ones in which they can come home after a day's battle to a loving wife and children, and home-cooked meals. As such, recruiting women into ISIS is not simply about expanding the organization. It is the essential building block of a future society. ISIS members have said their women do not fight, but are there to help build the new society.

In fact there are reports of significant numbers of women fighting for ISIS, including in an entire separate battalion of women fighters. Writing in *Foreign Affairs*, UN gender and conflict analyst Nimmi Gowrinathan described women fighters in ISIS within the historical context of women fighters in other violent movements:

> Living in deeply conservative social spaces, they faced constant threats to their ethnic, religious, or political identities – and it was typically those threats, rather than any grievances rooted in gender, that persuaded them to take up arms. ISIS' particularly inhumane violence can obscure the fact that the conflict in Iraq is also rooted in identity: at its base, the fight is a sectarian struggle between Sunni and Shi'a Muslims,

with several smaller minorities caught in between. It makes sense, therefore, that the all-female al-Khansaa Brigade of ISIS relies heavily on identity politics for recruitment, targeting young women who feel oppressed as Sunni Muslims. Indeed, anonymous fatwas calling for single women to join the fight for an Islamic caliphate have been attractive enough to draw women to ISIS from beyond the region.

Certainly the majority of people living in the so-called caliphate are local Iraqis or Syrians, held against their will by a violent movement controlling their villages or towns. But among those responding to ISIS recruiting efforts, the creation of the 'caliphate' as a physical place has drawn not only fighters but whole families to the territory under ISIS domination.

The *Washington Post* reported on how ISIS recruits families to its territory.

'The more they are successful at creating a whole new society, the more they are able to attract entire families,' said Mia Bloom, a professor of security studies at the University of Massachusetts at Lowell who has written extensively about women and terrorism. 'It's almost like the American dream, but the Islamic State's version of it.'

In the Syrian city of Raqqa, the group's main stronghold, the extremists have established a clinic for pregnant women run by a female gynecologist trained in Britain. Boys attend school, studying almost exclusively religion, until they are 14, when they are expected to start fighting, [British analyst Melanie] Smith said. Girls stay in school until they are 18; their instruction is about the Qur'an and sharia law, as well as learning how to dress, keep house, cook, clean and care for men, all according to a strict Islamic code.

Bloom said the Islamic State also appeals to women by providing electricity, food and a salary of up to $1,100 per month – a huge sum in Syria – for each fighter's family. The largesse is funded with money looted from banks, oil smuggling, kidnappings for ransom, and the extortion of truckers and others who cross Islamic State territory...

The United Nations has documented extreme brutality toward women by Islamic State radicals, including reports of women, particularly from minority groups, being stoned to death or sold into prostitution or sex slavery for its fighters.

But the Islamic State uses family imagery in its aggressive and highly polished online recruiting on social media, including videos showing fighters pushing children on swings and passing out toys, and children playing on bouncy castles and bumper cars, riding ponies, and eating pink cotton candy.

Certainly ISIS will not be able to maintain the reality of those illusory descriptions. But understanding the various reasons why some women might choose to support ISIS – the search for identity, wanting a sectarian or religious life, a sense of political or economic dispossession – remains as important in challenging ISIS influence as is the need to grasp the depth of the organization's attacks on women.

How did ISIS suddenly become so powerful? Why didn't anyone see it coming?

In 2014 ISIS was not new. It had been around at least since 2004, and had claimed its current name in 2011. But few outside of the region were paying much attention when this relatively small, relatively unknown organization suddenly swept across much of northern Syria, ignoring the border with Iraq and moving to occupy a huge swath of territory of western and central Iraq including Mosul, the second largest city in Iraq.

The ISIS announcement that it was establishing a caliphate, with the now-occupied Syrian city of Raqqa as its capital, was shockingly sudden and unexpected. That announcement was one reason new recruits from outside of Iraq and Syria, even outside the Middle East, began joining ISIS in much larger numbers. But the US response was most concerned with developments in

Iraq, where ISIS trampled the huge Washington-funded and Pentagon-trained military, whose soldiers and commanders mostly ran away, leaving their US weapons behind for ISIS to capture.

The immediate question was how ISIS was able to win what looked like such a lopsided battle. As Patrick Cockburn recounts in the preface to *The Jihadis Return*,

ISIS captured Iraq's northern capital, Mosul, after three days of fighting. The Iraqi government had an army with 350,000 soldiers on which $41.6 billion had been spent in the three years since 2011, but this force melted away without significant resistance. Discarded uniforms and equipment were found strewn along the roads leading to Kurdistan and safety. The flight was led by commanding officers, some of whom changed into civilian clothes as they abandoned their men. Given that ISIS may have had as few as 1,300 fighters in its assault on Mosul, this was one of the great military debacles in history.

So how could ISIS win, even temporarily, against powerful militaries in Iraq and Syria? There are two answers. In Syria, it was the chaos of an exploding civil war, with the regime's military stretched thin in some areas, and the anti-Assad opposition fighters – divided, poorly armed, and badly led – that allowed a better-armed, wealthier militia such as ISIS to move to a far more powerful position. There was simply too little opposition, and it was able to take over whole cities, such as its erstwhile capital, Raqqa, as well as sections of Aleppo and elsewhere, without serious opposition.

In Iraq, ISIS triumphed because it did not fight alone. It was able to take advantage of vital support from three components of Iraq's Sunni community, support shaped by the increasingly repressive actions of the Shi'a-dominated sectarian government in Baghdad. They included Sunni tribal leaders, Sunni former military officers including Saddam Hussein-era Baathist generals, and ordinary Sunni communities who bore the brunt of the US-backed Baghdad government's often brutal tactics.

Why did Sunnis support ISIS?

The reason for the Sunni support for ISIS had less to do with what ISIS stands for – many Iraqi (and Syrian) Sunnis are profoundly secular, and most remained very much opposed to the brutality of ISIS – and far more to do with the disenfranchisement of Sunni communities under the rule of Shi'a-controlled governments in Baghdad. For many, the ongoing repression at the hands of their own government made an alliance with ISIS an acceptable, even preferable option – despite, rather than because of, its extremism.

From the beginning of the US invasion and occupation of Iraq, the large Sunni minority had been at the forefront of opposition. Sunnis had been privileged under the Baathist rule of Saddam Hussein and held positions of power inside the government, especially in the military. All those positions were lost as the US occupation dismantled the civil service and destroyed the Iraqi army. Both before and after the creation of ISIS and its forebears, Sunni militias, some linked to tribal organizations and often led by former generals, played a huge role in fighting the US and the new US-created government and security forces being established in Baghdad.

The US-created Sunni Awakening, paying off Sunni militias to fight for the US and its allies rather than against them, worked for a while – the intensity of the civil war diminished. But the repression aimed at Sunni communities across Iraq never really ended during the Awakening movement's heyday, and when the US and Maliki stopped paying off the tribes, the repression escalated and Sunni opposition rose again.

Maliki's government had become a major part of the

problem of sectarianism in the country. As a consequence, Sunnis were far more likely to join with ISIS, seeing them as an armed force that would defend Sunni interests, or at least challenge some of the worst abuses of the Shi'a-led government. Despite the US having created the Iraqi government, and armed and funded it for more than a decade, by 2013 or so the Obama administration recognized that Maliki's sectarianism had become a major strategic threat to US interests.

Washington campaigned hard to get Maliki replaced in the 2014 elections, and that finally happened – but the result was disappointing. The new prime minister, Haider al-Abadi, was from Maliki's same Shi'a political party, and while his rhetoric tended to favour a more unitary and less sectarian approach, the ministries responsible for most of the repression (intelligence and defense) remained essentially unchanged.

And so did the Sunni resistance. The various components of Sunni support enabled ISIS to increase its strength and capacity. Some of the tribal leaders provided militia fighters to fight alongside, if not actually with, ISIS. In February 2015, National Public Radio noted that while the Sunni tribes are mainly in western Iraq,

you can also find them in neighbouring Jordan. Sheik Ahmed Dabbash, speaking from his house on a sleepy street in the capital Amman, says his tribe fought side by side with al-Qaeda against the Americans a decade ago... Now Dabbash's group is in a de facto alliance with ISIS. His views are typical of a broad spectrum of Sunnis in Iraq – Islamists, tribesmen, one-time supporters of Saddam Hussein. They feel victimized by Iraq's Shi'a-led government and many fight against the Shi'a-dominated army – either by joining ISIS or allying with them, even if they find the group extreme.

Those 'one-time supporters of Saddam Hussein' include military leaders, who may or may not have actually supported the former Baathist leader but who played key roles in the powerful Iraqi military. Those officers are widely believed to be providing both training and strategic planning for ISIS military campaigns. According to the *New York Times*, ISIS leader Abu Bakr al-Baghdadi's 'leadership team includes many officers from Saddam Hussein's long-disbanded army. They include former Iraqi officers like Fadel al-Hayali, the top deputy for Iraq, who once served Mr Hussein as a lieutenant colonel, and Adnan al-Sweidawi, a former lieutenant colonel who now heads the group's military council. The pedigree of its leadership, outlined by an Iraqi who has seen documents seized by the Iraqi military, as well as by American intelligence officials, helps explain its battlefield successes: Its leaders augmented traditional military skill with terrorist techniques refined through years of fighting American troops, while also having deep local knowledge and contacts. ISIS is in effect a hybrid of terrorists and an army.'

Even recognizing the *Times*' sloppy use of the term 'terrorist' – whose multiple definitions all start with attacking civilians or non-combatants, not an occupying army – it is clear that the unexpected military capacity of ISIS is bound up with the military training of former army officials of the Saddam Hussein era.

It is equally clear that changing the balance of power on the ground and reducing ISIS's power means severing the still-strong alliance between ISIS and Sunni communities and institutions. That will be difficult, perhaps impossible, as long as the US and its coalition continue large-scale bombing of ISIS targets in the midst of heavily populated Sunni cities, towns and regions, and as long as the Shi'a-led government in Baghdad continues its sectarian attacks on the Sunni community. The goal of winning Sunnis away from ISIS is undermined every time a US or Jordanian or British bomber or fighter-jet attacks Raqqa, for instance, or 'in ISIS-controlled Fallujah'. Both of those cities, in Syria and in Iraq, are heavily populated, and the likelihood of civilian casualties is almost inevitable. When US bombs are dropped and US policymakers cheer, Sunni Iraqis see it as another betrayal.

Because of the US military campaign, the claimed US goal of making new deals with Sunni tribes and winning over broader Sunni community support for the anti-ISIS struggle remains impossible to achieve. As NPR reported in February 2015, the 'US view on how to defeat ISIS involves making a deal with Sunnis like [tribal leader] Dabbash, and even incorporating their men into a sort of Iraqi National Guard. "The Guard is a breakthrough idea, because it will ensure that Iraqis are protected by people with whom they are familiar and in whom they have trust. It'll break down some of the sectarian divide," said US Secretary of State John Kerry. But that trust is sorely lacking among Dabbash and other Sunni leaders who have yet to show signs that they are ready to make a truce with the government in Baghdad.'

As long as they can count on support – or even lack of opposition – from Iraq's Sunni tribes, and as long as the multi-party civil war continues to rage across Syria, ISIS is likely to maintain its power at a level vastly disproportionate to its size.

Why are people from foreign countries joining ISIS and other extreme Islamist organizations in the Middle East?

There is a long history of foreign militants or wannabe militants travelling to the greater Middle East region to join Islamist campaigns. Perhaps the best known in recent years is the massive influx of foreign fighters who travelled to Afghanistan throughout the 1980s to join the indigenous *mujahideen*, or holy warriors, fighting against the Soviet Union at the height of the Cold War. One of the most famous of these was Osama bin Laden. The *mujahideen* were armed by the CIA, paid by Saudi

Arabia, trained by CIA allies in Pakistan's ISI intelligence service, and welcomed at the White House by President Ronald Reagan, who called them 'freedom fighters'.

More recently, foreign fighters travelled to Iraq to join various militias – including extremist Islamist groups, some of them linked to al-Qaeda – to fight against the US occupation. But the numbers were never enough to have a determinative impact on the military balance of power.

From the first months of the Syrian civil war, foreign activists arrived to support the anti-Assad opposition. As the initial nonviolent political campaign morphed into devastating civil war, many more arrived as humanitarian aid workers, driving ambulances, helping distribute international assistance. As the Islamist forces among the anti-Assad opposition rose in power and began to take over the major military roles from the secular democratic opposition, more Muslims from around the world arrived to join them. In some of the Islamist organizations, foreign fighters soon outnumbered Syrians.

In early 2015, the *New York Times* chronicled the wide range of reasons for the surge of potential fighters flocking to Syria to join the most extremist organizations. 'Young men in Bosnia and Kosovo are traveling to Syria for financial gain, including recruiting bonuses some groups offer, counterterrorism specialists say. Others from the Middle East and North Africa are attracted more by the ideology and the Islamic State's self-declared status as a caliphate. Counterterrorism specialists have seen criminal gang members from as far as Sweden seeking adventure and violence in the fight.'

There is no question that the process of embracing extremist Islamism very often begins in response to long histories of dispossession, disenfranchisement, exclusion and denial of rights among immigrant, Muslim or particular Islamic sects, and other minority communities in countries around the world. In the US, federal and state government policies are in place that continue to marginalize Muslim, Arab and other immigrant communities. Members of those communities, particularly young people, are often targeted during wars in the Middle East. President Obama acknowledged that 'engagement with communities can't be a cover for surveillance. It can't securitize our relationship with Muslim Americans, dealing with them solely through the prism of law enforcement.' But he didn't do or even propose anything to actually change the US and local state and municipal policies that do just this. Further, he made the statement at a conference designed to counter recruiting by ISIS and similar organizations, which was held a full seven months after he had ordered the bombing of Syria to begin.

In many European, American, and other Western Muslim communities, support for ISIS, al-Qaeda and other Islamist organizations exists despite, rather than because of, the violence of these groups. In 2013 and 2014, reports surfaced of European Muslims travelling to Syria to join ISIS with their entire families, babies and children included, to establish new lives in the so-called caliphate. At the end of 2014, the *Washington Post* profiled a British father, arriving in Syria to join ISIS with his family – his 'first four children had been born in London, his native city, but his new baby, wrapped in a fuzzy brown onesie, was born in territory controlled by the Islamic state'.

For many supporters from Western countries, the embrace of ISIS or other extremist organizations is often rooted in longstanding grievances at home. Those include permanent unemployment, discrimination, poverty, political dispossession, anger at rising Islamophobia, and the sense of not belonging to their country despite being born and raised there. Laws in Europe that prohibit hate speech are widely seen as perpetuating double standards, since they prohibit antisemitism but allow racist and Islamophobic slurs under the guise of free expression. Paris imam Mehdi Bouzid spoke of Cherif Kouachi, one of the *Charlie Hebdo* attackers, saying: 'We had lost him. Their message – the message [of radical Islam] – is tempting to those like Cherif. It promises them a place, acceptance, respect. They do not have that here.'

For some young people growing up in the squalid immigrant slums that surround many European cities, desperation and the lack of opportunity set the stage for often-petty criminal activity and sequential jail terms in violent prisons, which sometimes leads to indoctrination into some of the most radical versions of political Islam. Shortly after the *Charlie Hebdo* attack in Paris, the international press started paying attention to studies indicating that, as Reuters described it, 'prison radicalization is a problem in countries ranging from Britain and the US to Afghanistan. However, France stands out because over half its inmates are estimated to be Muslim, many from communities blighted by poverty and unemployment.' The disproportionate number of French prisoners who are Muslims, at 50 per cent compared to their estimated share of between 5 and 10 per cent of the population, reflects the same harsh reality that civil-rights attorney and author Michelle Alexander, in her seminal book *The New Jim Crow*, highlighted regarding African-Americans in US prisons: that the criminal justice system perpetuates racial inequality.

In one of the distinctions between ISIS and other jihadi organizations, including al-Qaeda, the declaration of a 'caliphate' has led ISIS to focus on recruiting professionals, such as doctors and engineers, and their families to come to live in this new quasi-state. Images of family life in the 'caliphate' form part of slick, web-based recruiting campaigns. In Raqqa, the ISIS 'capital' in Syria, thousands of local residents have been forced out, their homes distributed to ISIS fighters, supporters and their families, who also receive money, electricity and healthcare. Reportedly, education for children – boys and girls – is available, shaped by the ISIS version of Islam and sharia law. At the same time, extreme brutality – toward local civilians, particularly women, non-Muslims, anyone who opposes ISIS rule, anyone who differs from the ISIS leadership's fanatical interpretations of Islam – remains the norm.

Is the typical ISIS fighter a Muslim of Middle Eastern descent?

Not all foreign supporters are coming from Western countries. As an imprisoned Saudi human rights activist told the *Washington Post*: 'So many Saudis are engaged with the Islamic State because of the lack of political freedoms in our country. They are frustrated because they cannot express themselves.' Describing young prisoners being recruited to join the Islamic State, he said: 'It's like committing suicide for them to join the Islamic State, but they feel that their lives don't matter because of the injustice in this country. That's what happens when people are deprived of their rights.'

But throughout 2014, reports also began to surface regarding young people, mainly Europeans, who were either almost secular, non-practising Muslims or not Muslim at all, choosing to join ISIS or other violent organizations because of alienation or other reasons unrelated to religious extremism. As the author of *Inside British Islam*, Innes Bowen, told *Business Insider* magazine: 'There was no single type of person who becomes a radical in the UK, and no single pathway to their ideology. There must be a range of motivations – a sense of adventure, a misplaced sense of duty or idealism – some of those recruited are well versed in ideology and the politics of their radical cause, others are surprisingly ignorant.' Numerous press outlets reported the story of young recruits in Europe who purchased *Islam for Dummies* and *The Koran for Dummies* on Amazon before leaving for the Middle East.

The assumption that most would-be terrorist recruits are likely to be practising Muslims, most likely from an

Arab or other immigrant background, and somehow identifiable through racial and religious profiling, needs to remain suspect. A classified 2008 report from Britain's MI5 that was leaked to *The Guardian* acknowledged that,

> Far from being religious zealots, a large number of those involved in terrorism do not practise their faith regularly. Many lack religious literacy and could... be regarded as religious novices... The MI5 analysts concluded that 'a well-established religious identity actually protects against violent radicalization...' British-based terrorists are as ethnically diverse as the UK Muslim population, with individuals from Pakistani, Middle Eastern, and Caucasian backgrounds. MI5 says assumptions cannot be made about suspects based on skin colour, ethnic heritage or nationality... The researchers conclude that the results of their work 'challenge many of the stereotypes that are held about who becomes a terrorist and why'. Crucially, the research has revealed that those who become terrorists 'are a diverse collection of individuals, fitting no single demographic profile, nor do they all follow a typical pathway to violent extremism'.

While circumstances – particularly the rise of social media – have certainly changed since 2008, the notion that terrorists are most likely to come from particular communities that can be identified by law enforcement needs to be continually challenged.

2 The global war on terror

What is the 'global war on terror'?

One day after the September 11 attacks on New York's
World Trade Center and the Pentagon in 2001, then-
President George W Bush announced that the US
response to this crime would be to lead a global war on
terror.

The first target was Afghanistan, despite the fact
that none of the 19 hijackers responsible for the attack
were Afghans (they were Saudis and Egyptians), none
of them lived in Afghanistan (they lived in Hamburg),
none went to flight school in Afghanistan (they went
to flight school in Florida), none trained in Afghanistan
(they trained in Minnesota). But the leaders of al-Qaeda,
the organization the hijackers were linked to, had found
refuge in Afghanistan, which was then under the rule
of the extreme Islamist Taliban government. Using the
language of 'bringing those responsible to justice', the
Bush administration launched a war of aggression that
soon stretched far beyond Afghanistan, in countries
with no connection to al-Qaeda, targeting nonexistent
organizations and individuals who were still children
when the Twin Towers were attacked.

That war continues today – some call it Permanent
War.

Since 9/11, the US has gone to war in Afghanistan
and Iraq, in the Philippines and Libya, Somalia, Yemen,
Djibouti, Saudi Arabia, Syria, and beyond. For much of
the world the war was defined by CIA-run 'rendition',
in which people were snatched off the streets, smuggled
to so-called black sites around the world, or to the
Pentagon-run prison at Guantánamo Bay, and subjected
to years of detention without trial, and interrogation
using a limitless range of torture techniques. Among
Americans, initial support for the Afghanistan 'war on
terror' was based on cries for vengeance. Bush told a

stunned and frightened nation that the choice the US faced was to either go to war or let them get away with it. And since letting the perpetrators 'get away with it' was an unacceptable option, the vast majority of Americans chose war. On 7 October, weeks after the attacks, the US launched a massive air and ground war against Afghanistan, overthrowing the Taliban government and bombing vast stretches of the impoverished country. Tens of thousands of Afghans were killed. At the height of troop deployments, 100,000 US forces and tens of thousands more NATO troops occupied Afghanistan. More than 14 years later, thousands of US troops were still in Afghanistan, in what had long ago become the longest war the United States ever fought.

What is terrorism?

Terrorism has no single definition. The word is politically charged and its meaning is rarely agreed upon. Well over 100 definitions of the word exist in different countries, among different organizations, and under varying sets of laws.

US law requires the State Department to report to Congress every year on terrorist attacks around the world. It defines terrorism as 'premeditated, politically motivated violence perpetrated against noncombatant targets by sub-national groups or clandestine agents.' That definition might sound objective and neutral, but it leaves lots of questions unanswered. Who are 'noncombatant' targets? Not the same as civilians, apparently, since the attacks on the armed warship USS Cole, the US Marine Corps barracks in Beirut, the Pentagon and other military installations are routinely referred to as 'terrorist' attacks. Does it mean soldiers are noncombatants if they're sleeping, or just not on patrol at that moment? Then there's the confusion over the 'sub-national groups or clandestine agents' part. Does that mean 'state terrorism' is not a recognized reality, or might 'clandestine agents' include agents of a state, to explain the common US references to 'Iranian terrorist attack'? If noncombatants – real noncombatants, like civilians – are deliberately attacked by national, not sub-national groups, like the Israeli Air Force in Gaza for instance, in a 'premeditated, politically motivated' campaign, is that exempt from the term 'terrorism'?

What are the implications of the world's inability to agree on a definition of terrorism?

In the absence of a coherent definition, 'terrorism' tends to be used almost exclusively to describe political violence committed by extremist Muslims. It's a term used to create fear and to justify repressive actions, whether in the United States or in the context of the 'global war on terror'.

Often in the United States an act of 'premeditated, politically motivated violence' is assumed to be an act of terror, rather than the result of mental illness or some other possible cause, when the perpetrator is Arab or Muslim. For example, following the 2009 deadly attack on soldiers at Fort Hood, Texas, by Major Nidal Malik Hasan, the question of Hasan's mental state was never addressed. In incidents when the perpetrator is white, the term 'terrorism' is carefully avoided, and mental illness is often asserted as the most likely cause, as was the case in the 2011 attack on Representative Gabrielle Giffords in Tucson, Arizona. Similarly, 'an argument over a parking space' was claimed as the reason a white neighbour killed three young Muslim Americans in North Carolina in 2015, despite the killer having expressed hatred of Islam and other religions and having threatened the victims earlier by displaying his guns.

Similarly, whether an act perpetrated by Muslims abroad is deemed terrorism by the United States also depends on *which* Muslims are held responsible. In official US circles, for example, the beheadings routinely carried out by the Saudi government as part of a judicial system designed to terrify political opponents are never referred to as terrorist acts, but ISIS beheadings are routinely identified as proving the terrorist nature of the organization.

In early 2015, Saudi Arabia passed a new law that defined any form of political opposition as terrorism. Saudi King Abdullah, who died in January 2015, had already declared that political dissidents were terrorists no different from violent organizations, and that atheism equalled terrorism. Just days after Abdullah's death, the Saudi government announced a new anti-terrorism law, of which Article One defined terrorism as 'calling for atheist thought in any form, or calling into question the fundamentals of the Islamic religion on which this country is based.'

The foregoing examples demonstrate that the definition of 'terrorism' and 'terrorist' depends on who is using the term, supporting the common notion that 'one person's terrorist is another person's freedom fighter'. Nelson Mandela was placed on the US 'anti-terrorist' list in 1988 by then-President Ronald Reagan, who excoriated the revered South African leader as a communist during the Cold War. Long after his 1990 release from prison, and even when he was elected president of South Africa in 1994, Mandela remained on that list. It took until 2008 for his name to finally be removed.

In US federal criminal law, 'international terrorism' is defined as violence or acts dangerous to human life that appear to be intended 'to intimidate or coerce a civilian population; to influence the policy of a government by intimidation or coercion; or to affect the conduct of a government by mass destruction, assassination, or kidnapping.' This definition doesn't limit terrorism to attacks by non-state actors.

Ambassador Edward Peck, a retired US diplomat with experience throughout the Arab world, described on *Democracy Now*! his work as deputy director of the White

House Task Force on Terrorism under then-President Ronald Reagan. The task force, he said, was asked

> to come up with a definition of terrorism that could be used throughout the government. We produced about six, and in each and every case, they were rejected, because careful reading would indicate that our own country had been involved in some of those activities... After the task force concluded its work, Congress [passed] US Code Title 18, Section 2331... the US definition of terrorism... [O]ne of the terms, 'international terrorism,' means activities that, I quote, 'appear to be intended to affect the conduct of a government by mass destruction, assassination or kidnapping...' Yes, well, certainly, you can think of a number of countries that have been involved in such activities. Ours is one of them... And so, the terrorist, of course, is in the eye of the beholder.

How did the fight against al-Qaeda in Afghanistan shift to Iraq?

Afghanistan was never the main target. Vice-President Dick Cheney, Defense Secretary Donald Rumsfeld, and others leading the Bush administration's war drive, particularly the heavily represented neoconservative ideologues staffing the Vice-President's office and the Pentagon, had Iraq in their sights from the moment the planes hit the Twin Towers. Pretexts for going to war against Iraq abounded: phony assertions regarding self-defence, made-up allegations that Iraqi leader Saddam Hussein had ties to al-Qaeda, forged documents about Iraq purchasing yellow-cake uranium from Niger, fictitious reports of aluminium tubes from China that could 'only' be used to build nuclear weapons, sham warnings of Iraq's supposed stockpiling of weapons of mass destruction.

All were false, and an unprecedented global anti-war movement arose, climaxing on 15 February 2003, when record-breaking crowds of between 12 and 14 million people filled streets across the globe, united around the slogan 'The World Says No to War'. Protests were launched in more than 665 cities, with the largest reserved for Italy, Spain, and Britain, whose leaders had agreed to join Bush's imminent war despite overwhelming popular opposition. The breadth and depth of the protests moved the *New York Times* to acknowledge on its front page that 'there may still be two superpowers on the planet: the United States and world public opinion'. Unwilling to give in to US pressure, a wide range of governments backed the street protests. So did the United Nations Security Council, which stood firm for eight months against US and British pressure to endorse the coming war.

But plans to attack Iraq were already under way, and not even a worldwide outcry could prevent it. The Pentagon, backed by British forces, launched the invasion and occupation of Iraq on 19 March 2003. Within a month, US troops overthrew the Iraqi regime.

What were the consequences of the overthrow of Saddam Hussein?

The US forces disbanded Iraq's military and dismantled Iraq's government, seizing power in occupied Iraq in the name of the Coalition Provisional Authority (CPA). The CPA was made up of thousands of US bureaucrats, most of them chosen more for loyalty to the Bush administration than for any experience in the vast and disparate areas of governance they controlled. The CPA was itself backed by billions of dollars and hundreds of thousands of US occupation troops, as well as thousands of 'coalition' troops and Pentagon-paid military mercenaries. Hundreds of thousands of Iraqi troops, including most of the generals, were unceremoniously dismissed. Hundreds of thousands of Iraq's government officials and civil servants, most of whom had been required to sign on to the ruling Baath Party to get their job, were sent packing in the name of 'de-Baathification'. Anger and opposition to the occupation rose immediately, with supporters of the old regime, nationalists of various stripes and many ordinary Iraqis mobilizing political as well as military resistance.

A year later the CPA was replaced by an interim Iraqi government, which provided Iraqi faces in government posts but was still appointed by and dependent on the US occupation. Washington created new political parties, all based on sectarian identities. Ostensibly they were designed to reflect the relative size and power of Iraq's various religious communities. Under Saddam Hussein's Baath Party, many Sunni Iraqis had found access to elite positions in the military, business and elsewhere, while majority Shi'a in many cases were discriminated against, or at least were denied privileged financial and social status. With the overthrow of the government, that position was reversed, and the majority Shi'a emerged as the most powerful political force. They were strengthened by the many Iraqi exiles who had spent years as refugees in Shi'a Iran or in the West, and were now returning with strong US backing. But as Iraqi national identity was forcibly abandoned in favour of the smaller and narrower categories of Sunni, Shi'a, Christian, Kurd, Turkoman, Yazidi, etc, sectarian conflict began to rise.

The US occupation of Iraq remained the centrepiece of Bush's 'global war on terror'. As a result, an entire population, already suffering from decades of war and 12 years of crippling economic sanctions that had shredded much of the country's social fabric, now faced the devastation of full-scale war. Under the new Shi'a-dominated Iraqi government that the US backed, parties based on religion recruited their own militia forces, and the war took on an increasingly sectarian cast. The US occupation forces created and perpetuated the new system, although Shi'a-led militias were among a range of forces fighting against the US.

As is the case in any foreign military occupation, resistance was both broad and deep, including militias and resistance forces from across Iraq's crazy-quilt population. There were armed supporters of Sunni tribal leaders, Shi'a militias with close ties to Iran, former Baathist-led secular forces, and widely diverse and popular resistance organizations. As the occupation extended over years, an increasingly extremist sectarian resistance grew, and a civil war erupted alongside the anti-US resistance, pitting Sunni against Shi'a.

3 The new global war on terror

What were the origins of the 'new' global war on terror?

In June 2014 ISIS, which had re-emerged under its new name in 2011 (see Part I, 'ISIS'), began an escalated military campaign, seizing major cities both in Syria (Raqqa), and in Iraq (Mosul, the second-largest city in the country). In response, the United States sent thousands of troops back into Iraq and began airstrikes over Syria. The second edition of Washington's global war on terror was under way.

President Obama came into office pledging to end what he called the 'dumb' war in Iraq, but also promising to pay more attention to – read 'escalate' – the supposedly 'good' war in Afghanistan. He did both. (It should be noted that the final troop withdrawal from Iraq – originally negotiated by George W Bush – was not in fact the President's choice. Obama tried and failed to persuade the Iraqi parliament to grant impunity to US occupying troops after 2011; if he had succeeded, thousands of them would not have been withdrawn at all.)

In his first months in office in 2009, President Obama immediately escalated the US presence in Afghanistan, sending first 17,000 and then 33,000 additional troops there. By October 2015 about 10,000 of those troops remained. Obama announced he was reversing his withdrawal-in-2016 plan and instead would keep those troops in Afghanistan, continuing combat, training and special operations until the end of his term in office. Obama joined the European-initiated NATO air assault on Libya in 2011, and throughout his presidency he has escalated drone strikes in Yemen and Somalia and continued strikes in Pakistan and Afghanistan. In September 2014 thousands of US troops were back in Iraq for training and special operations, and US warplanes were bombing ISIS, Nusra Front and other targets in Iraq and Syria. In

February 2015 the *New York Times* editorial board called it 'Washington's new war in the Middle East', and three months later, the US announced publicly that its special forces were indeed on the ground in Syria killing and capturing alleged ISIS militants.

In fact, the earlier edition of the global war on terror never really ended. Some of the same reasons for the war remain – issues of oil, stability, military bases, and strategic reach across the broader Middle East are still important. Military response is still the default position when the public or policymakers pressure the powers that be to 'do something'.

But the global war on terror was always about shaping public opinion in the United States as well as carrying out the war itself. And by the time of the temporary withdrawal of all US troops from Iraq at the end of 2011 and the significant reduction of US troop numbers in Afghanistan under way during that same period, together with the reduced public awareness of the escalating drone attacks, the power of the 'global war on terror' paradigm to shape America's overall role in the world had, for a time, begun to diminish.

President Obama quickly rejected Bush's phraseology, but he continued the global war on terror in practice. He eventually settled on a more dispassionate-sounding handle to describe the wars raging in Iraq and Afghanistan, as well as his less publicized drone and assassination wars. The Pentagon's office of security review made it official in a May 2009 email to Defense Department staff, which stated, '[T]his administration prefers to avoid using the term "Long War" or "Global War on Terror". Please use "Overseas Contingency Operation".'

There were other differences too. Under Obama, the White House and the Pentagon were not led by neo-conservative extremists with an ideological commitment to using war for regime change and to expand US influence around the world. There are numerous strategic differences between the administrations as well, including on questions of where the war is fought, who and what are the targets, who is defined as the 'enemy', the relative reliance on drones and reluctance to use large-scale ground forces. But ultimately, Obama's version of the global war on terror has largely continued in the same vein as his predecessor. Regardless of who was in the White House, the war has clearly never succeeded in any of its ostensible goals, whether ending the threat of terrorism or bringing pro-American stability, development, and maybe even democracy to conflict-ridden and human rights-denying (but resource-rich) countries.

Obama continued the use of military force as a supposed answer to terrorism, but he had campaigned against the Iraq war, and was widely seen as reluctant to embrace the full-scale use of force. His agreement to go to war in Libya came only in response to pressure from supporters of 'humanitarian intervention' in the State Department, including then-Secretary of State Hillary Clinton, National Security Adviser Susan Rice, and UN Ambassador Samantha Power. He came close to attacking Syria directly in 2013, but pulled back in the face of the loss of British support and of massive anti-war mobilization at home. This was not a Bush-style administration in which ideologues eager for war held every powerful seat in the Departments of State and Defense as well as the White House.

Bush's first request to Congress for an authorization for the use of military force (AUMF), just two days after 9/11, allowed the President to use 'all necessary and appropriate force against those nations, organizations, or persons he determines planned, authorized, committed, or aided the terrorist attacks that occurred on September 11, 2001, or harbored such organizations or persons, in order to prevent any future acts of international terrorism against the United States by such nations, organizations or persons.'

It contained no restrictions as to place, kind of weapons, concern for civilians, or length of time. The authorization was for global, endless war. Only one member of Congress, Representative Barbara Lee of California, voted against the resolution. (Other members have since said that their biggest regret in Congress was having voted for the use of force.) A separate AUMF was passed approving war in Iraq in 2002; again it contained no limits as to time, place or anything else. Even though the White House eventually requested a new authorization specific to ISIS, it did not fight for or win such authority and the Obama administration maintained the claim that at least the 2001 and maybe the 2002 AUMFs provided sufficient authorization for its use of force in Syria and Iraq in 2014.

In 2010 and 2011, as US troops were being pulled out of Iraq and the war in Afghanistan stalled, President Obama seemed to shift toward greater engagement with some Islamist governments and political forces. While the wars, particularly the assassination and drone war, continued at the same pace, a closer US alliance with Turkey's Islamist-leaning government emerged. Then, when the Arab Spring erupted at the end of 2010, the Obama administration began a cautious shift away from some longstanding pro-US dictatorships. It moved to recognize, if not embrace, some of the Islamist parties and leaders who came to power through popular uprisings in which they were allied with broad secular coalitions, including leftist and labour, women's rights and human rights organizations, as well as pro-Western political forces and ultimately parts of the military.

In Tunisia, the White House leaned toward new openness to, if not actual support of, the Islamist (often described as 'moderate Islamist') Ennahda Party, which won early elections after the overthrow of the country's US-backed Zine el Abidine Ben Ali, who had ruled with an iron fist for almost a quarter-century. As protests spread across Egypt in January 2011, then-Secretary of State Hillary Clinton reaffirmed US support for longstanding US-armed and -funded dictator Hosni Mubarak, saying,

'Our assessment is that the Egyptian government is stable and is looking for ways to respond to the legitimate needs and interests of the Egyptian people.'

But as the uprising of Tahrir Square broke out, with millions of Egyptians filling the streets, the administration relented. After some days of refusing to relinquish support for Mubarak, the White House, however reluctantly, called for Mubarak to step down. It later recognized, though never supported, the democratically elected President Mohamed Morsi, who came to power with the backing of the Muslim Brotherhood, the largest component of the broad secular-religious movement that had swept away Mubarak's legitimacy and pushed the military into deposing him.

It's unclear whether that tentative shift toward recognition of Islamist social forces might have slowed the US drive to war. But the shift never reflected an all-sided split from traditional US strategic goals – even the recognition of Islamist-oriented governments was still based on Washington's search for regional pro-US stability rather than any commitment to democracy or representation of all sectors of Arab society. In any event, the shift was not to last.

Even as the US recognized President Morsi, the $1.8 billion of US aid to Egypt continued to flow from the Pentagon directly to the Egyptian military, bypassing the government. When Egypt's military carried out its brutal (though unfortunately popular in some secular circles) anti-Morsi coup in the summer of 2012, the US continued its military-to-military relationship as if nothing had changed. The tentative feints toward a closer relationship with the democratically elected, Islamist-oriented government in Turkey soon faded, and the traditional relationship – 'NATO ally but not a close one' – re-emerged.

As Islamist forces rose to the most influential and powerful positions in the anti-Qadafi uprising in Libya and the once-democratic and secular anti-Assad rebellion in Syria, the US found itself fighting on the same side as some of the most brutal Islamist forces in the region. Yet it still claimed, against an increasingly visible reality, to be allied only with the secular and 'moderate' forces, not the Islamists.

Obama continued to resist acknowledging that he was commanding a widening war in the Middle East. It was the renewed pressure for just such a full-scale war against ISIS in 2014 that brought the 'global war on terror' back to public attention. So this is not really a new war but rather a re-energized and escalated one, with renewed airstrikes against targets in Iraq and Syria, a new commitment to send thousands of US troops back to Iraq, cancellation of plans to withdraw troops from Afghanistan, and an Obama administration effort to gain congressional authorization for the use of force against ISIS. (As before, if the White House has its way, that authorization will have no limits on geographic scope, breadth of targets, or years of validity.)

How did the overthrow of Qadafi in Libya lead to ongoing conflict there?

In 2011, what began as a nonviolent political challenge to the erratic dictatorship of Muammar al-Qadafi in Libya quickly morphed into an armed effort to overthrow the regime. With the regime's brutal response to the protests as a pretext, NATO quickly agreed to requests by Europe and then the US to intervene militarily. The US/NATO air assault, authorized by the United Nations Security Council for humanitarian protection only, immediately (as predicted) turned into another military campaign of regime change in the Middle East. Qadafi was overthrown, captured and murdered, and the country descended into a maelstrom of competing militias. Extremist Islamist forces emerged among the most powerful, and the regime's vast arsenal of weapons disappeared from warehouses only to reappear throughout the country and across Libya's borders to fuel new – mainly Islamist – insurgencies across Africa and the Middle East. The Libyan weapons continue to fuel Washington's opponents in the global war on terror.

What was the significance of the fall of Mosul?

As Patrick Cockburn, perhaps the best Western journalist working in the broader Middle East, described it in his seminal book *The Jihadis Return: ISIS and the New Sunni Uprising*, 'the "war on terror", the waging of which has shaped the political landscape for so much of the world since 2001, has demonstrably failed. Until the fall of Mosul, nobody paid much attention.'

When Mosul, Iraq's second-largest city, was overrun by ISIS in June 2014, the US-trained, US-armed, and US-paid Iraqi military largely fled the advance of a few thousand ISIS fighters, leaving behind most of their weapons. ISIS then imposed its extreme version of Islam, and devastating hardships, upon the people of Mosul. After Mosul, President Obama's version of the global war on terror was reborn and re-energized, with US troops back to Iraq, renewed US bombing in Iraq, and the expansion of bombing and on-the-ground special forces raids in Syria. Weapons from post-Qadafi Libya, brought about by the US-NATO air war in 2011, flooded the region, many of them turning up in the hands of ISIS fighters. Many more civilians were killed – many by ISIS and still more under US bombs. It was after 'the fall of Mosul,' in Cockburn's words, but while a lot more people were paying attention, the new global war still wasn't helping the people forced to live under ISIS rule.

How effective have the Obama administration's strategies been in this new war?

President Obama stated his official goal in the new global war on terror plainly: 'Our objective is clear: we will degrade, and ultimately destroy [ISIS] through a comprehensive and sustained counterterrorism strategy.' But there is a huge disconnect between that goal and the action the administration is taking.

Obama began using that language in early September 2014, just as he was launching the US bombing of Syria and returning US troops to Iraq. At just about the same time, according to a classified document quoted later in the *New York Times*, Major General Michael K Nagata, commander of US special forces in the Middle East, confessed: 'We do not understand the movement [ISIS], and until we do, we are not going to defeat it. We have not defeated the idea. We do not even understand the idea.'

That was quite an admission. Understanding one's perceived enemy must always be the first step in deciding what to do about it. The close proximity of 'we don't understand' and 'we're sending the troops and the bombs' provides a good indication of why the goals of 'degrade and destroy' have not been achieved. Rather, the US military involvement has left ISIS intact and to some degree even stronger than before.

By the time the *Times* wrote about Nagata's efforts to understand the terrorist organization, months into Obama's military campaign, ISIS was expanding, not collapsing, under the bombs. When the bombing of Syria and Iraq began in September 2014, the White House had said its stated goal was to destroy the headquarters of the violent and extremist ISIS. But you can't bomb extremism out of existence. The US had tried that with al-Qaeda in Afghanistan and it didn't work there either. By 2010 the CIA admitted that only somewhere between 50 and 100 Afghan fighters were left in all of Afghanistan, though nearly 100,000 US troops remained in the country. The bombing campaigns had killed some fighters and forced many more to flee across Afghanistan's borders, but the organization's offshoots had already started taking root in a host of neighbouring countries.

The same thing is happening with ISIS. On 30

September 2014, Vice News reported: 'Coalition warplanes launched a fresh wave of airstrikes against Islamic State targets across Syria on Saturday, despite demonstrations in the town of al-Atareb condemning the US-led assault, which residents have blamed for the deaths of at least 27 people, including civilians, in the area. The protests in al-Atareb on Friday brought together dozens of people who marched and chanted through the streets, some holding placards. One sign written in English read: "Don't kill our children by your aircrafts". The outcry from residents comes three days after coalition forces conducted joint drone and plane strikes against a militant base. The bodies of at least 27 locals were pulled out of the rubble, including an unspecified number of civilians, according to a report from a group called the al-Atareb Civil Defense.'

The bombs the US dropped did not land on 'extremism', they fell on al-Atareb, or on Raqqa, a 2,000-year-old Syrian city with a population of more than a quarter-million people: men, women and children who had no say in the ISIS takeover of their city. The Pentagon reported the bombing of targets like a post office and the governor's compound, so the likelihood of a large number of casualties among civilians unable to flee was almost certain, although with Raqqa still under ISIS control it is not possible to confirm casualty numbers.

US airstrikes and bombing have not brought about any strategic defeats of ISIS. The Syria bombing began in Kobane, for example, in September 2014, following graphic media coverage of the ISIS assault on the city, just over the border with Turkey. The US launched its bombing campaign in response to the humanitarian disaster, which appeared nightly on high-definition video streamed directly from cameras on the Turkish side of the border, available to every television and social media platform in the world. Yet just a couple of weeks into the bombing campaign, Secretary of State John Kerry announced in a public speech that Kobane was not even a 'strategic objective' for the US.

In its January 2015 issue, *Mother Jones* magazine, noting Kobane's lack of strategic significance, asked and answered the question, 'So why all those bombs?'

> Since September 23, when air strikes in Syria began, US and coalition forces have pummeled both Syria and Iraq with nearly 2,000 air strikes. As of early this week, 870 of those strikes were in Syria; almost 70 per cent of these Syrian strikes have focused on Kobane and its surroundings. The total area, about the same size as Rhode Island, covers less than two per cent of Syria and the majority of the population are ethnic Kurds.
>
> There's a reason that Kobane became so symbolically important: stories of the brave Kurdish fighters defending the small border city against ISIS swept international headlines last September, and the public demanded that the US step in to prevent a humanitarian disaster. The Kurds, unable to defeat ISIS on their own, turned the tide once they had coalition air support. 'Seventy-five per cent of all US strikes in Syria were on Kobane,' Thomas Pierret, a Syria specialist at the University of Edinburgh told *Ekurd Daily*, a Kurdish news site last week. 'You give any force on the ground that kind of aerial support and they will get the upper hand.' It has cost taxpayers $8.2 million a day, on average, to conduct the entire airstrike campaign.

By January 2015, ISIS was mostly pushed out of Kobane. Victory was declared. It was another example of what used to be called 'the CNN factor' (but might today be known as the Twitter factor): a media-driven public demands that the government 'do something', usually defined as something military, and the government accedes to that demand. But, as *Mother Jones* noted at the time, 'ISIS now occupies one-third of Syria, or twice what it did when the campaign began, and around 400,000 people have fled Kobane alone. US military officials have conceded that Kobane isn't strategically important.'

By the time the US was ready to make that admission, the damage had been done. As *Al Jazeera* reported, 'tens of thousands of Syrian Kurds who fled their homes due to fighting in Kobane have returned to find at least half of the town destroyed, Kobane officials said... Rafaat al-Rifai, reporting from Kobane, said destruction was visible everywhere, especially in places where ISIL fighters were based and later targeted by US-led air strikes.' The twisted logic of Vietnam could be applied once again to Kobane: 'It became necessary to destroy the town to save it.'

What was behind the US decision to escalate its direct military involvement in Middle East conflicts in 2014?

The question remains as to why the United States chose – and it was a choice, not a necessity – to resume direct engagement in the global war on terror after several years of winding down US troops and airstrikes in favour of an expanded drone war fought from afar. The horrific up-close-and-personal violence of ISIS, its imposition of draconian punishments and a legal system rooted in the seventh century, even its capture of swaths of territory, all made the terrorist organization dangerous to people living under its control. But that didn't make it a threat to the US.

In early September 2014, just as the US bombing resumption and troop return was being prepared, the outgoing head of the National Counterterrorism Center, Matthew Olsen, said 'there is no credible information that [ISIS] is planning to attack the United States,' and there is 'no indication at this point of a cell of foreign fighters operating in the United States – full stop.'

So why were some influential Washington voices so eager to go to war in Syria and to return to Iraq? For some, regime change against all of the Middle Eastern states that rejected Washington's domination – Iraq, Syria, Iran

(Libya was perhaps a bonus) – remained a continuing commitment. They and others recognized that Iran was the most important Middle East power remaining hostile to US and Israeli interests, and Tehran was the key regional supporter of the Assad regime in Damascus. So in the early part of the Syrian civil war, US actions against Syria were aimed less at going after the Syrian regime for its own sake than at weakening Iran by undermining its most important Arab ally. Few voices urged greater US military engagement primarily to protect Syrian or Iraqi civilians – if that happened, it would be a side effect, useful for mobilizing public support.

Until about May 2013, Obama was leading the faction of his administration that was very reluctant to participate directly in the Syrian civil war. Despite incremental US military involvement – sending 500 CIA agents to train rebel fighters in Jordan, helping Turkey 'facilitate' weapons transfers to make sure they went to the 'right' rebel forces, and allowing (perhaps encouraging) Saudi Arabia and Qatar to send US weapons directly to rebel forces – Obama himself seemed unwilling to go further. There was no rising majority in Washington for a no-fly zone, for arming the rebels directly, or for airstrikes against Syrian missile defences.

But the pressure continued from political forces who had long wanted the US to support regime change in Damascus and from the anti-Iran contingent. The shift for the administration came in August 2013, with the (still unproven) claim that Bashar al-Assad was responsible for a chemical weapons attack in the outskirts of Damascus. The media coverage showing graphic evidence of the attack helped push a previously war-averse public toward a renewed demand that the US 'do something'. The pro-war officials and their counter-parts among the rightwing think tanks, the punditry and the media escalated the pressure as well, and the Obama administration relented, threatening to go to war directly in Syria.

Still, a majority in the US opposed or at least were hesitant about entering a new war in the Middle East, and the Obama administration faced the risk of significant opposition from the president's political base. A decision by the British parliament, enabled by a re-energized anti-war movement, to reject joining the US in a Syrian war allowed Obama to pivot toward Congress to decide. In response, a massive anti-war mobilization immediately took shape in the US, pressuring Congress and ultimately forcing the administration to accept a face-saving arrangement initiated by Russia. A new escalation to a US war in Syria was averted – temporarily.

How did the US justify its return of troops to Syria and Iraq?

A year later, officially in response to the crisis facing the Syrian Yazidis besieged by ISIS on Mount Sinjar, the new war was officially launched. That war, to 'degrade and destroy ISIS', has largely failed. ISIS continues to control huge swaths of territory and millions of people, despite the US and allied airstrikes killing what the Pentagon in June 2015 estimated may be up to 10,000 ISIS fighters (along with an unknown number of civilians). ISIS still occupies and rules Mosul, Iraq's second-largest city, as well as the Syrian town of Raqqa and beyond. By mid-October 2015, ISIS had captured a string of towns and villages just north and close to striking distance of the ancient Syrian city of Aleppo.

In his January 2015 State of the Union address, President Obama said his goal was to diminish the primacy of the military overseas. 'When we make rash decisions,' he said, 'reacting to the headlines instead of using our heads; when the first response to a challenge is to send in our military – then we risk getting drawn into unnecessary conflicts, and neglect the broader strategy we need for a safer, more prosperous world. That's what our enemies want us to do.'

He was absolutely right. The problem was that his policy responding to the ISIS crisis, beginning in August 2014, was precisely what he warned against: It was a rash decision, it was driven by headlines, it privileged immediate military action while only mentioning non-military options in passing. It drew the United States into an unnecessary conflict and was exactly what ISIS wanted. And it not only neglected the broader strategy, it rendered much of it impossible – closing the Guantánamo Bay prison becomes much less of a priority while US troops are on the ground and US bomber pilots are above the skies over Iraq and Syria.

Later in his speech Obama bragged that 'in Iraq and Syria, American leadership – including our military power – is stopping ISIL's advance. Instead of getting dragged into another ground war in the Middle East, we are leading a broad coalition, including Arab nations, to degrade and ultimately destroy this terrorist group. We're also supporting a moderate opposition in Syria that can help us in this effort, and assisting people everywhere who stand up to the bankrupt ideology of violent extremism.'

But the reality was starkly different. Neither American leadership nor anything else was stopping the advance of ISIS, as demonstrated by ISIS gains in Ramadi and Palmyra in 2015. Far from avoiding 'another ground war in the Middle East', the US was already in another ground war, with thousands of troops back in Iraq. In February 2015 Secretary of State John Kerry made clear his view that the door should be left open for ground troops in Syria as well. And a month later, the chair of the Joint Chiefs of Staff, General Martin Dempsey, said he would not rule out sending US ground troops into Syria.

The 'moderate opposition' in Syria used to mean what the US described as secular and generally pro-Western armed anti-Assad rebels, but most of them have either collapsed or joined ISIS or one of the other not-so-moderate opposition forces. And as for 'people everywhere who stand up to the bankrupt ideology of violent extremism,' in Obama's words, in Iraq that would mean primarily Iran along with the Shi'a militias it supports, which in early 2015 played the largest military role in defeating ISIS in Tikrit. While the US-led coalition and Iran remained on opposite sides in Syria regarding protection of vs opposition to the Assad-led regime, both were still opposed to ISIS. The Iran deal signed later that year between Tehran, Washington and other world powers could set the stage for building further rapprochement between the US and Iran as a basis for new diplomacy to end the Iraq war.

Have US airstrikes stemmed the growth of ISIS and al-Qaeda?

Every bomb the US drops recruits more supporters. As the Pentagon-linked RAND Corporation noted in March 2013, the 2003 American invasion of Iraq 'provided al-Qaeda with a new front, a new recruiting poster, and a new destination for global jihadists'. The Chatham House research organization in London reported that the war 'gave a boost to the al-Qaeda network's propaganda, recruitment and fundraising.' Today's ISIS fighters will likely see the same boost in morale and enrolment from US planes dropping bombs and from US troops coming back on the ground, even if some military targets are destroyed and some ISIS supporters (or their families) killed.

The US military is not stopping ISIS. In fact the influence of ISIS, if not its actual organization, is growing as US airstrikes continue. In February 2015 the *New York Times* reported that ISIS was 'expanding beyond its base in Syria and Iraq to establish militant affiliates in Afghanistan, Algeria, Egypt and Libya, American intelligence officials assert, raising the prospect of a new global war on terror. Intelligence officials estimate that the group's fighters number 20,000 to 31,500 in Syria and Iraq. There are less formal pledges of support from "probably at least a couple hundred extremists" in countries such as Jordan, Lebanon, Saudi Arabia, Tunisia and Yemen, according to an American counterterrorism official.'

Such reports are likely severely exaggerated – 'a couple hundred extremists' does not make a global terrorist organization. Even the *Times* article itself acknowledged that it was unclear 'to what extent this is an opportunistic rebranding by some jihadist upstarts hoping to draft new members by playing off the notoriety of the Islamic State.'

It is far from certain that pledges of loyalty to ISIS from small groups of jihadis, or even from larger organized groups that may indeed pose a local threat, such as Boko Haram in Nigeria, represent anything close to a real increase in ISIS's threat. But claims of ISIS expansion – many of them becoming front-page stories in major US newspapers – do ratchet up the fear factor among the US public. A similar phenomenon occurred during George W Bush's global war on terror. Abu Sayyaf, a violent but quite tiny gang of criminal thugs in the southern island of Mindanao in the Philippines, explained their violence in an Islamist framework. In a claim accepted unequivocally by the mainstream US press, the Bush administration upgraded the status of the gang to that of the just-discovered Southeast Asian branch of al-Qaeda, leading to a vast escalation in US military involvement in the Philippines. That was, of course, before extremist organizations had come to use the internet and social media to issue their own declarations. But the relative truth of the claims of ISIS connections remains equally suspect.

US intelligence analysts told the *New York Times* in March 2015 that 'it remained unclear what specific fighting capabilities, if any, the relationship [with ISIS] would add to Boko Haram, or how soon'. But by that time the US had already significantly increased its military presence in Africa. The *Times* reported more than 200 US special operations troops training local forces just in West Africa, plus Air Force Reaper surveillance drones supporting on-the-ground French military actions in Niger and Mali. Significantly, the US military escalation also included Navy SEALS training Nigerian commandos – not to go after Boko Haram, but 'for action in the oil-rich delta' where the Nigerian government has histori-cally collaborated with Western oil companies in a savage military campaign against the indigenous population and environment of the Niger Delta.

Whether or not any of the US actions under way in Africa have anything to do with ISIS remains uncertain. What is in fact clear is that more than a year of airstrikes that have killed thousands of ISIS fighters, along with unknown numbers of civilians, has not stopped ISIS from advancing in Iraq and Syria. That should not be surprising. Fourteen years of airstrikes and ground war in Afghanistan didn't conquer extremism, or even eliminate al-Qaeda or the Taliban. Twelve years of fighting (in the most recent US war) in Iraq didn't overcome extremists or bring about inclusive or democratic governance. There's no reason to think years of more US fighting in Syria and Iraq or in Egypt and Libya – or Yemen, Somalia, Pakistan or the other far-flung battlefields of the global war on terror – will lead to any better results. The danger is that US reliance on military action first – and most of the time, military action only – will be expanded far beyond the current war theatre to any country where militants of any sort, threats to the United States or not, decide to claim, for reasons of pride or propaganda, some version of the name ISIS for their own.

Are drones playing a different role in this war than they did during the Bush years?

George W Bush used drones in both Afghanistan and Iraq from the beginning of the wars. He also ordered a relatively small number of drone attacks in Pakistan and Yemen. But under Obama, the use of drones in the US war on terror has vastly expanded, both in intensity and geography, with the drone war conducted far beyond the 'official' war zones of Iraq and Afghanistan.

Bush's first drone strike outside of Afghanistan was in Yemen in November 2002. Then there was a break of 18 months, until June 2004 when the first CIA-run drone attack hit Pakistan.

According to the Bureau of Investigative Journalism (BIJ) in London, by the time Obama took office in January 2009, Bush had carried out 51 drone strikes outside of Iraq and Afghanistan, killing between 410 and 595 people, of whom 167 to 332 were civilians, including 102 to 129 children.

Obama left that record in the dust. The BIJ determined that, as of October 2015, there had been more than nine times more strikes under Obama in Pakistan, Yemen and Somalia than there were under his predecessor, George W Bush. Obama ordered his first drone strike only three days into his presidency. Since then, US drones have killed at least 2,577 people outside the declared war zones – including Pakistan, Yemen and Somalia – of whom at least 488 were civilians.

While drone strikes continue to kill in Afghanistan – terrorists, 'militants', civilians and children among the victims – the massive expansion of the drone war in countries far from those official war zones, combined with the explicit use of drones for specific assassinations, is perhaps Obama's signature war strategy. The Pentagon conducts drone strikes in Afghanistan (even if based on CIA-compiled intelligence and planning), so these are not kept quite as secret as the CIA drone campaigns elsewhere.

Obama's early choice of the drone war strategy reflected his recognition that, along with growing outrage regarding the war in Iraq, longstanding public support for the war in Afghanistan was quickly eroding as well. A weapon that could guarantee that no US casualties would occur – only people 'over there' would be killed – would fit easily into that reality. Drones were the perfect weapon for a war based on American exceptionalism.

What are the pros and cons of using drones versus troops on the ground?

Even putting moral issues aside, the military value of drone strikes remains suspect. Five months into Obama's first term, noted counterinsurgency expert David Kilcullen and Andrew Exum of the Center for New American Security wrote an op-ed in the *New York Times* describing the use of drones, particularly in Pakistan. 'This is similar to what happened in Somalia in 2005 and 2006, when similar strikes were employed against the forces of the Union of Islamic Courts. While the strikes did kill individual militants who were the targets, public anger over the American show of force solidified the power of extremists. The Islamists' popularity rose and the group became more extreme.'

Then, as if anticipating those who later chose, however reluctantly, to support ISIS, they wrote: 'While violent extremists may be unpopular, for a frightened population they seem less ominous than a faceless enemy that wages war from afar and often kills more civilians than militants.'

In the United States, as more information emerged regarding the Obama administration's reliance on drones, including in the assassination of American citizens, and the existence of Tuesday-morning White House meetings devoted to updating the 'kill or capture' list, the drone war became a focus of growing anti-war pressure. Debate arose over why Obama, a legal scholar who seemed light years from the Bush administration's disdain for the rule of law, chose to rely so heavily on a tactic so clearly in violation of international law.

In a February 2011 *Newsweek* article titled 'Inside the Killing Machine', Tara McKelvey writes: '[s]ome counterterrorism experts say that President Obama and his advisers favor a more aggressive approach because it seems more practical – that administration officials prefer to eliminate terrorism suspects rather than detain them. "Since the US political and legal situation has made aggressive interrogation a questionable activity anyway, there is less reason to seek to capture rather than kill," wrote American University's Kenneth Anderson, author of an essay on the subject that was read widely by Obama White House officials.'

So apparently Obama administration pragmatism, combined with both public outrage over torture and Obama's inability to close the prison at Guantánamo Bay, meant that killing suspects instead of capturing them was simply deemed easier for all concerned. And drone strikes were by far the quickest, cheapest, and easiest method for such assassinations, even if they were not nearly as accurate as was claimed.

How has Obama expanded the drone war?

Later in 2011, documents released by WikiLeaks indicated that the US was launching drone attacks against both Yemen and Somalia from a base in Djibouti on the northwest African coast, and the US was planning another drone base in Ethiopia.

Obama's expansion of the drone war was not only geographic but also increased the number of potential targets. Originally aiming drones at specific, identified individuals – extra-judicial assassination, already way outside the bounds of international law – the administration soon created a particularly frightening version known as 'signature' strikes. This meant that any person or group of people acting in a certain way, or present in a particular area, would be considered appropriate targets for drone strike because of their 'signature' actions.

While the White House has claimed it no longer relies on such tactics, it has done nothing to repeal the self-granted permission to use them. The *New York Times* reported in 2012 that when Obama 'applies his lawyering skills to counterterrorism, it is usually to enable, not constrain, his ferocious campaign against al-Qaeda – even when it comes to killing an American cleric in Yemen, a decision that Mr Obama told colleagues was "an easy one".'

The assassination of American citizens also pulled the drone war into public view. A February 2013 document leaked to NBC News created new outrage, although perhaps not as much as might have been anticipated. It was a memo from Obama's Department of Justice, outlining the

> legal framework for considering the circumstances in which the US government could use lethal force in a foreign country outside the area of active hostilities against a US citizen who is a senior operational leader of al-Qaeda or an associated force of al-Qaeda... Here the Justice Department concludes only that where the following three conditions are met, a US operation using lethal force in a foreign country against a US citizen who is a senior operational leader of al-Qaeda or an associated force would be lawful: (1) an informed, high-level official of the US government has determined that the targeted individual poses an imminent threat of violent attack against the United States; (2) capture is infeasible and the United States continues to monitor whether capture becomes feasible; and (3) the operation would be conducted in a manner consistent with applicable law of war principles.

Constitutional protection, due process, the right to a trial would be abandoned. International legal prohibitions against targeted assassination would be ignored. And the drone war would be the framework for carrying out this newly 'legal' authority – all rooted, we were told, in the 2001 Authorization for the Use of Military Force, which Bush had brought to Congress three days after the 9/11 attacks.

What are the immediate effects of the drone war?

Even putting aside considerations of morality and law, the effect of the drone strikes is devastating. The *New York Times* reported that 'Mr Obama's ambassador to Pakistan, Cameron P Munter, has complained to colleagues that the CIA's strikes drive American policy there, saying "he didn't realize his main job was to kill people" a colleague said.' It went on to note that 'drones have replaced Guantánamo as the recruiting tool of choice for militants; in his 2010 guilty plea, Faisal Shahzad, who had tried to set off a car bomb in Times Square, justified targeting civilians by telling the judge, "When the drones hit, they don't see children".'

In his 2015 State of the Union address, President Obama said he wanted to impose 'prudent limitations' on the drone war. But the only limit that would be remotely 'prudent' would have to involve ending the drone war. It violates US and international law, kills civilians, foments more terrorism, and doesn't make anyone safer either in the US or in the countries where the strikes are aimed. The president admitted 'we will not be safer if people abroad believe we strike within their countries without regard for the consequence.' The problem, of course, is that the hallmark of Obama's drone war is precisely that the US *does* exactly what 'people abroad believe' – striking in their countries without regard for the human, legal, or moral consequences. The only way to solve the problem is to *stop* the drone war altogether – not just to strike more prudently.

Instead, a month after his speech, the Obama administration announced it would for the first time allow the almost unlimited export of armed drones. The administration crafted a set of principles for recipient countries, many of which have some of the worst human rights records in the world, but those principles are unlikely to have much impact on the longstanding practice of governments like those in Saudi Arabia,

Bahrain or others. The new policy, as the *New York Times* described it, would be 'a delicate balancing act for the Obama White House, which has sought to elevate human rights in its foreign policy but also has employed drone strikes like no other government in history.'

That balancing act became even more precarious in late April 2015, when a CIA drone attack targeting alleged al-Qaeda operatives in Pakistan killed two Western hostages, American development expert Warren Weinstein and Italian aid worker Giovanni Lo Porto. President Obama apologized to the families, but maintained, according to the *Wall Street Journal*, that 'the initial US assessment of the strike shows it was fully consistent with the guidelines under which his administration conducts such counterterrorism operations.'

In October 2015, *The Intercept* published a set of articles based on a newly leaked cache of classified documents detailing the US drone-based assassination programme: 'Documents detailing a special operations campaign in northeastern Afghanistan, Operation Haymaker, show that between January 2012 and February 2013, US special operations airstrikes killed more than 200 people. Of those, only 35 were the intended targets. During one five-month period of the operation, according to the documents, nearly 90 per cent of the people killed in airstrikes were not the intended targets. In Yemen and Somalia, where the US has far more limited intelligence capabilities to confirm the people killed are the intended targets, the equivalent ratios may well be much worse.'

The source came from within US intelligence agencies, and included classified Pentagon documents. Noted earlier whistleblowers Daniel Ellsberg and Edward Snowden both welcomed the documents' release as an important step towards greater transparency, and rights groups including the American Civil Liberties Union and Amnesty International called for independent investigations of the assassination programme.

4 The Syrian war in the global war on terror

What is the war in Syria all about?

The Syrian uprising that began in early 2011 was part of the broader regional rising that became known as the Arab Spring. The particular origins and later trajectory of Syria's uprising were also rooted in a terrible drought that was a direct result of climate change, lack of irrigation and human-caused desertification. It affected about 60 per cent of Syrian land and had hit Syria's agricultural production from at least 2007. According to the United Nations, in the first two years alone about 1.3 million people were affected and over 800,000 lost their entire livelihood. As more and more farmers were driven off their land, unable to survive, they flooded the cities looking for work. But, as in so many places, job scarcity meant that the few jobs available were likely to go to those who knew someone in power. In Syria it was the Alawites, the long-privileged minority group that included the ruling Assad family, who held sway.

The result was that non-Alawites, most of them majority Sunnis, were less likely to find work, causing a rise in sectarian tensions. Modern Syria had not been a particularly religious country; the Alawite-dominated government had always been ruthlessly secular. But secular or not, it had created a system of economic and political privilege for Alawites. The identity-based politics and privilege were very real, so the new pressures caused by the economic consequence of the climate crisis led to an upsurge in sectarian divides and antagonisms.

At the beginning of the uprising, Syria's nonviolent protesters poured into the streets with political/democratic demands that broke open a generations-long culture of fear and paralysis. They did not initially call for the overthrow of the regime of President Bashar al-Assad, but for massive reforms and an end to the terrible repression.

It is important to recognize the crucial divergence between the role the Assad regime has played domestically and its perceived regional position. As *Jadaliyya* co-editor Bassam Haddad wrote, 'most people in the region are opposed to the Syrian regime's domestic behaviour during the past decades, but they are not opposed to its regional role. The problem is the Syrian regime's internal repression, not its external policies.' That could describe the view of many Syrians as well.

Assad was not, like the leaders in Egypt and Tunisia, a US-backed dictator. His domestic policies were brutal, though he remained popular among some sectors of the Syrian population. In the region, Assad served as the self-proclaimed leader of the region's supposed anti-Western arc of resistance. That contradiction led some global activists to support the Syrian government as a bastion of anti-imperialism and therefore to condemn all opposition forces as lackeys of Washington.

Such a position of course denied Syrians political agency in their own country, including the right to rise up against a repressive government. But Syria's assumed regional resistance role was far from a complete reality as well. Based on its alliance with Iran (and somewhat for its support of Hizbullah in Lebanon) the US clearly viewed Syria as an irritant. But Damascus has never been a consistent opponent of US interests. In 1991 the first President Assad, Bashar's father Hafez, sent warplanes to join the US coalition attack against Iraq in Operation Desert Storm. After 9/11 the US collaborated with Bashar al-Assad to send innocent detainees to be interrogated and tortured in Syria.

As for Syria's supposed anti-Israel role in the region, despite the rhetorical and diplomatic antagonism between the two, Syria had been a generally reliable, predictable and often useful neighbour for Tel Aviv. For example, in 1976 Damascus backed a murderous attack by rightwing Falangists and other Christian militias against the Palestinian refugee camp at Tel al-Zaatar during Lebanon's civil war. Overall, the occasional border clash or small-scale eruption of violence aside, Assad had kept the border, and thus the strategic and water-rich Golan Heights, illegally occupied by Israel since 1967, largely quiescent.

The uprising that began in early 2012 had everything to do with the Syrian government's domestic repression, not its regional or international role. It started with a group of teenage boys in Dera'a, who wrote slogans against the regime on public walls. They were caught, viciously beaten, and tortured in prison. A mass protest movement was the response. At first the protesters did not call for the overthrow of the regime, nor were they calling for the militarization of their struggle or for international military intervention. The Assad government responded with brutal force and then promised a set of reforms. But it never delivered.

It was defectors from the Syrian military who first took up arms in response to the regime's brutal suppression of the initially nonviolent protests. In July 2012, a year into the increasingly militarized struggle, one of the early political opposition leaders, Michel Kilo, said: 'If this destruction goes on and the ruling regime wins, it will rule over ruin and thus suffer a strategic defeat. If the opposition wins, it will inherit the country in an unmanageable condition. In any case, it is necessary to stop this violence, stop this bloodshed.'

The US and its allies, like some but not all of the Syrian opposition, rejected any negotiations that were not based on Assad stepping down as a precondition to any talks. The military battles escalated, and the defensive use of arms quickly morphed into a network of militias and fighters, largely unaccountable to anyone and unco-ordinated among themselves, who began carrying out attacks on security forces and calling for international military assistance. It would soon transform the Syrian uprising into a full-scale civil war, as well as what UN Secretary General Ban Ki-moon in August 2012 described as a 'proxy war' in which the 'acts of brutality that are being reported may constitute crimes against humanity or war crimes'.

Some of the secular opposition militias formed a coalition known as the Free Syrian Army, or FSA, with a political wing, the National Coalition for Syrian Revolution and Opposition Forces, based originally in the tiny Gulf state of Qatar. The US and some of its allies agreed to provide money and arms if the disparate militias united under a single organization. But unity among the various fighting groups, and between the FSA and the coalition, was never achieved, and tensions were exacerbated as competing outside forces, primarily in the region but global as well, began to champion various factions as proxies for their own interests. The US provided some training by CIA teams in Jordan and 'non-lethal' military aid, but the Obama administration initially balked at large-scale military support. US allies in the region, particularly Saudi Arabia, Turkey, Qatar and the UAE, moved much more quickly to provide funds, weapons and access to illicit border crossings to arm and supply the various militias. In September 2014 Washington officially agreed to provide more and bigger weapons, more training and more money to the opposition. Soon after, the US initiated direct airstrikes –against ISIS and the Nusra Front, not against the regime – inside Syrian territory.

The war claimed huge numbers of victims; by January 2015 the UN reported 220,000 people killed. Although many reports often assumed that almost all the dead were civilians and that the Assad regime was responsible for virtually all the violence of the war, the reality was that most of the victims were actually military, and the largest number were supporters of the regime. In June 2013 the Syrian Observatory for Human Rights reported that civilians accounted for 37 per cent of the casualties. By January 2015 the percentage of civilians killed had dropped to 24 per cent.

The civil war in Syria seems so complicated – is it really just one war?

Initially a political, largely nonviolent popular uprising against a repressive regime, the Syrian civil war became a military conflict that morphed into at least eight separate wars, mainly proxy battles for outside players. They all involved governments within and outside the region that provided money and arms, with some also involving outside fighters, and direct military participation. Whatever the level of outside involvement, these wars were being fought to the last Syrian.

The first was the original civil war that pitted large sectors of the Syrian population – first nonviolent political opposition movements and later armed militias of various sorts – against the regime of Bashar al-Assad. During the first years, many, though certainly not all, of Syria's businesspeople as well as numerous minority communities, including the Alawites, other Shi'a, Christians, Druze, some Kurds and others, tended to side with the government. The Assad regimes, from 1970 through at least 2015, had long protected those minority groups, especially privileging the Alawites. With the erupting civil war, many of those Syrians feared the possibility of a takeover by the majority Sunnis and saw the government as a safer bet despite its brutal treatment of political opponents. The Assad government was armed and backed by Russia and Iran. As the war dragged out for years, and especially with the destruction of much of Aleppo, Syria's business centre, by both government and opposition attacks (including by ISIS), business support for the regime diminished. The escalating war also destroyed many of the original nonviolent political activists and organizations that had first challenged the regime, with many imprisoned, dead, injured, or forced into exile; by mid-2013 their voices had been largely suppressed by the violence of the war.

Second was the regional war for hegemonic power, largely between Saudi Arabia and Iran. The other wealthy pro-US oil states of the Gulf – Qatar, Bahrain and the UAE – along with Jordan, Turkey and Egypt after the overthrow of elected President Mohamed Morsi, sided with Saudi Arabia (although Qatar and Saudi Arabia competed for influence in Syria as well, backing separate Islamist factions). Iran was backed by the Shi'a Hizbullah party and militia in Lebanon, as well as by the Syrian regime itself.

Third was the sectarian war for regional influence, involving the same forces as those above, but shaped around the Sunni-Shi'a divide in the Middle East. Saudi Arabia, backed by the tiny Gulf petro-states, was joined by Egypt, Jordan, and Turkey in a Sunni arc backing the Syrian rebels – 'moderate' and Islamist alike. Their Shi'a opponents, led by Iran with the support of Iraq and the powerful Lebanese militia Hizbullah, are standing by the Syrian government. This does not mean that all these governments are attempting to create theocratic states based on their own dominant sects. The governments in Syria and Iraq, for instance, were always ruthlessly secular. But the al-Assad family, which has dominated Syria since 1970, is Alawite (an offshoot of Shi'a Islam). So, when the jobs and perks that come with state power were available for distribution, the Alawite community often received first pick, and then began trying to protect their privileges by allying themselves with other minorities – Christians, Druze, and others – against the Sunni majority. It was this war that attracted most of the foreign and primarily Sunni jihadist fighters to Syria. They had little interest in supporting Saudi Arabia's government (and in fact most jihadi organizations from the 1970s and 1980s initially emerged to challenge the Saudi monarchy as insufficiently devout), but participating in a war in which Sunni jihadists were winning some victories against the Shi'a/Alawite 'infidels' proved to be a powerful draw.

Fourth was Syria as another venue for the war between the US and Israel on the one side and Iran on the other. Until the rise of ISIS in Syria and its dissolution of the border between Syria and Iraq, Iran's role as arms supplier and strategic backer of the government in Damascus was the primary reason for US interest in Syria. Iran is the most important Middle East power that remains hostile to US and Israeli interests, including opposition to Tel Aviv's nuclear weapons monopoly in the Middle East. With the rise of ISIS, Syria has become more important as a US target in its own right. But with Tehran still relying on its strategic alliance with Assad, the US maintained its goal of weakening Iran by undermining its most important Arab ally. By late 2014 that effort had been further complicated by Iran's new role against ISIS, with Tehran backing the Iraqi government and providing, with Russia, the most important military and economic support to the Syrian government. Iran's opposition to ISIS was consistent with its earlier opposition to the pre-ISIS Syrian rebels. The difference now was that Iran's opposition to ISIS put it into a significant, if unspoken, partnership with the US. The nuclear deal reached in July 2015 between Iran and the 'P-5 + 1' (referring to the five permanent members of the UN Security Council plus Germany) represented a significant victory for diplomacy over threats of war. But it remained unclear whether the US was prepared to use the easing of relations with Iran to move towards broader negotiations over Syria. One example was evident in the reluctant ambiguity of Secretary of State John Kerry over accepting Iranian participation in the Vienna talks he organized with Russia, Saudi Arabia and Turkey in October 2015.

The fifth war positioned Syria as the key Middle East arena of global competition between the US and Russia for regional military/strategic power and influence. Moscow's hold on its naval base at Tartus, on Syria's southern Mediterranean coast, is a key reason for its support for the Syrian government, just as Washington remains committed to the port in Bahrain that hosts the Pentagon's Fifth Fleet. Russia will fight for its Tartus base to the last Syrian, just as the US will do anything, including arming and supporting the 2011 Saudi-UAE military intervention against peaceful Bahraini protesters, to keep its Fifth Fleet in place. US-Russian competition for the region's resources – especially control of oil and natural gas pipelines that could either bypass Syria (aiding US allies) or go through Syria (helping Russia and its allies) – also fuels the conflict. The US-Russia tension played a particularly damaging role in the failed 2012 effort to convene multilateral negotiations to end the Syrian crisis. When Russia escalated its involvement to direct military engagements – including airstrikes and limited ground troops – in October 2015, Moscow and the US quickly arranged military-to-military contacts for 'deconfliction', or the avoidance of attacking each other. They agreed on targeting ISIS but, while the US was backing opposition fighters also targeting the Assad regime, Moscow maintained that the Syrian military remained the key factor preventing an ISIS takeover of Syria, and thus expanded its attacks beyond ISIS to include other anti-Assad forces, targeting al-Qaeda's Nusra Front as well as other Islamist and some Western-backed opposition fighters.

The sixth war emerged as a battle between the secular and Islamist forces within the anti-Assad opposition. This became increasingly brutal in 2013 and 2014, as powerful Islamist militias either sidelined or, in many cases, attacked secular anti-Assad forces in order to seize territory or, more often, to seize weapons. The Free Syrian Army (FSA) and other secular forces, some of which were vetted and deemed 'moderate' by the US, were provided with significant arms. They promised to maintain control of those weapons, including undertaking to 'record the serial number' of every weapon, but it quickly became clear that they had no military capacity to prevent the weapons from falling into the hands of the better-armed ISIS and other Islamist forces, which were also often more disciplined and better trained. In fact many secular Syrian fighters themselves defected and joined the Nusra Front and other Islamist militias, including ISIS, desperate to join what looked like a winning (and more reliably salary-paying) side against the Assad government.

By late 2013, the seventh war had emerged, this time as a battle within the Islamist forces themselves. It pitted a variety of Islamist groups, most notably the al-Qaeda-linked Nusra Front, against the brutal ISIS militia, and was fought over weapons and territory that had been wrested away from the regime.

The eighth war took shape when Turkey moved from facilitating arms and opposition fighters crossing its border into Syria to playing a direct military role – beginning in July 2015 when Ankara agreed to allow US warplanes to fly out of the Incirlik airbase and initiated its own airstrikes inside Syria. But Turkey's military involvement was much more complicated, as it simultaneously engaged against Kurdish targets, especially in Iraq. Those targets were primarily of the militant nationalist Kurdish Workers Party or PKK, with whom Ankara's two-year-old ceasefire collapsed that summer. Turkey's involvement was thus rooted in a host of internal political issues as much as in Ankara's opposition to Assad, but its escalation further complicated the already convoluted sets of military players in the Syrian war.

What was the story behind the chemical weapons attack that led President Obama to threaten to bomb Syria in 2013?

By June 2013 the civil war in Syria had expanded, with civilians being killed, injured and dispossessed in huge numbers. Discussions were under way about an international peace conference, but they weren't getting very far. Even as the US and Russia continued talking about such a meeting, arms shipments from and to all sides continued to threaten even greater escalation.

Arms, mainly US arms, were flowing to Syrian rebel forces from Qatar, the UAE, and Saudi Arabia via Turkey and Jordan as well as directly from the US. Britain and France forced the European Union to end its prohibition on sending arms to the opposition, and the US cheered the EU decision. Russia announced it was sending Damascus advanced anti-aircraft missiles and Israel threatened to bomb those missiles if they arrived in Syria.

 Starting early in 2013, pressures began to mount on the Obama administration to engage even more directly in Syria, to establish a no-fly zone, create 'safe corridors' for rebel forces, send heavy weapons to the US-identified 'good guys' among the rebels, train additional rebels beyond those the 200 CIA agents in Jordan were then training, even to conduct direct airstrikes on Syrian targets. All were on the wish list of the 'we want to attack Syria and we want to do it now' voices in Congress, the punditry and beyond, who advanced numerous reasons why the US should go to war, including claims of chemical weapons being used by the Syrian regime, but without evidence to back up the claims.

President Obama resisted the pressure. But his defiance was weak and cautious. We don't have enough evidence yet, White House officials said on numerous occasions. It's not clear the red line has been crossed. The clear implication was that if there *was* more evidence, if some claimed red line *was* crossed, then all bets would be off.

It wasn't clear that the enormous costs – in US taxpayers' money and in Syrian lives – would have been a sufficient deterrent. And the diplomatic rhetoric maintained the ominous 'all options are on the table'.

By the summer of 2013, the political pressure began to rise again. On 21 August, reports surfaced of a poison-gas attack against civilians in the suburbs of Damascus, the Syrian capital. What was clear was that it was a horrific attack, with hundreds of people, including many children, dead and injured. What remained unclear and unconfirmed was almost everything else, including how many had died and, crucially, who was responsible.

Initial reports from activists on the ground said about 300 people had been killed. The international aid organization Médecins Sans Frontières reported at least 3,600 patients with 'neurotoxic' symptoms at hospitals it supported, of whom 355 died. The Syrian Observatory for Human Rights said it had confirmed 502 deaths. French intelligence sources said the figure was at least 281 deaths. And the US claimed that 1,429 people had been killed. The huge disparity in casualty figures has never been fully explained. There were reports that the US number included all the people who had been killed in the area around Ghouta and nearby Baghdad suburbs within the same three-day period as the chemical attack, meaning many who were killed by other weapons by unknown forces would have been included in the numbers. But that was never confirmed.

The United Nations sent inspectors shortly after the attack to determine the nature of the chemical and the kind of weapons used to disseminate it. They confirmed sarin gas had been used, but they were not mandated to determine who was responsible. Even before the UN or any investigation had begun, US officials immediately asserted that the Syrian regime had launched the attack. Human Rights Watch carried out its own investigation and reached the same conclusion based on the trajectory of rockets involved in the attack.

But other sources soon raised serious questions about the validity of the assumption that the Syrian government was the only possible culprit. Associated Press reported that Washington officials were punching holes in the administration's allegations. Then a widely read investigation by the award-winning journalist Seymour Hersh in the *London Review of Books* demonstrated significant weaknesses in the White House claims. Hersh wrote:

> Barack Obama did not tell the whole story this autumn when he tried to make the case that Bashar al-Assad was responsible for the chemical weapons attack near Damascus on 21 August. In some instances, he omitted important intelligence, and in others he presented assumptions as facts. Most significant, he failed to acknowledge something known to the US intelligence community: that the Syrian army is not the only party in the country's civil war with access to sarin, the nerve agent that a UN study concluded – without assessing responsibility – had been used in the rocket attack. In the months before the attack, the American intelligence agencies produced a series of highly classified reports, culminating in a formal Operations Order – a planning document that precedes a ground invasion – citing evidence that the Nusra Front, a jihadi group affiliated with al-Qaeda, had mastered the mechanics of creating sarin and was capable of manufacturing it in quantity. When the attack occurred Nusra should have been a suspect, but the administration cherry-picked intelligence to justify a strike against Assad.

For many, though rarely given voice in the mainstream media, the insistence that only the Assad regime could have been the perpetrator, that none of the other military forces in the country (including military defectors and Islamist extremists) could have stolen or produced sarin, echoed the Bush administration's insistence on claims of Baghdad's weapons of mass destruction to justify the invasion and occupation of

Iraq 10 years earlier. The issue shifted quickly from the attack itself to how the US might respond. The Obama administration immediately began using the language of 'red lines'. The Syrian government's use of chemical weapons, we now heard, meant it had crossed a red line and now US military intervention would be on the agenda. The double assumption was that first, the Syrian regime was the known culprit, and second, that 'red lines' mean only military options are available, that diplomacy has no role to play. Just a week after the chemical attack, the US began moving troops and other military assets into position 'just in case'. The *Wall Street Journal* quoted an anonymous 'senior defense official' who said the military strikes being considered 'would be conducted from ships in the Eastern Mediterranean using long-range missiles, without using manned aircraft. "You do not need basing. You do not need over-flight. You don't need to worry about defenses."'

Domestic pressure from Congress, pundits and much of the press continued to rise. Britain, Turkey, and Germany all indicated support for some kind of military action. By early September Israel joined the demand, although it had previously not called for a military assault on Syria, partly because the Syrian regime, despite its 'resistance' rhetoric, had historically been very useful to Israel. But Prime Minister Netanyahu and others appeared to fear that if there were no US military strike against Syria, Iran would draw the conclusion that Tehran's crossing of a supposed 'red line' some time in the future might not result in a military strike either.

Why didn't the US attack Syria over the chemical weapons issue in 2013?

There were numerous impediments to going to war. Neither side of the war debate in Washington seriously took into account that the escalating crisis in the Middle East was taking place simultaneously with a significant decline of US influence. With US economic and diplomatic power reduced, military force remained the one arena in which the US was the indisputable champ. But even 2013's $800-billion US military budget could no longer determine history by itself. For example, US participation in the 2011 NATO campaign in Libya was partly, though not entirely, an attempt to remilitarize the US role in the region and thus reassert US centrality. But whether or not US policymakers were prepared to acknowledge it, that military intervention, like its predecessors in Iraq and Afghanistan, had already failed. And whether or not they were prepared to anticipate or acknowledge it, military intervention in Syria was certain to fail as well.

A major political problem for US policymakers was that an arms embargo, a necessary component of any serious diplomatic alternative, would also hurt some of their most important campaign contributors: the arms dealers. Despite the increasing recognition that military intervention has failed, the US remains the largest arms exporter in the world; sending US arms to one side of Syria's civil war (and thus extending the war) helped to justify things like Washington's then-pending $10-billion joint arms sale to Israel, Saudi Arabia, and the UAE. Instability in Syria, whatever its cause, would help reinforce calls for increasing the existing $30-billion, 10-year commitment of US military aid to Israel to an unprecedented $47 billion. Calling for an arms embargo was never going to be easy.

There was also the problem of the fundamental illegality of any US military escalation. There are only two conditions in which a military attack by one country against another (including establishment of a no-fly zone) can be legal: either it is authorized by the UN Security Council or it is a case of immediate self-defence. Neither condition existed. The Council had been burned in 2011 after approving the use of force in Libya. The US and its allies had promised that the assault would be limited to humanitarian protection but instead, as many had predicted, it immediately turned into a war for regime change. Two years later, the Security Council was certainly not going to repeat that mistake, so there would be no UN authorization. And there was no way even the most hawkish warmongers in the US could claim that Syria's civil war represented an immediate national threat to the US. Any US attack – with or without a congressional mandate – would have been a clear violation of international law.

There was also the problem of cost. In July 2013, then-Chair of the Joint Chiefs of Staff, General Martin Dempsey, testified in the Senate that creating a no-fly zone in Syria would cost over a billion dollars per month. He said that a bombing campaign designed, officially, to hit 'high-value' targets inside Syria would mean sending hundreds of warplanes, Navy ships, even submarines. Even the more limited military goal of trying to gain control of Syria's chemical-weapons stockpile would, Dempsey said, require thousands of Special Forces and many other troops on the ground. Perhaps having learned at least a few of the lessons of the disastrous wars in Afghanistan, Iraq, and most recently Libya, Dempsey acknowledged that: 'We have learned from the past 10 years, however, that it is not enough to simply alter the balance of military power without careful consideration of what is necessary in order to preserve a functioning state.'

The US government was clearly divided. On the one hand, it allowed the false dichotomy to stand, claiming the only two options were either a military strike or 'we let 'em get away with it'. The White House did not present alternatives for other kinds of international accountability, such as investigation by the International Criminal Court. Rumours circulated that, knowing that UN authorization was impossible, the US might ask NATO for approval of a military strike against Syria, recalling the Kosovo precedent of 1999. (The problem was that, in

2013 as in 1999, the UN Charter was very clear on what constituted a legal use of military force – and permission from NATO was not on that very short list.)

On the other hand, even President Obama had acknowledged that attacking Syria would mean violating international law. Two days after the chemical attack he said: 'If the US goes in and attacks another country without a UN mandate and without clear evidence that can be presented, then there are questions in terms of whether international law supports it... and those are considerations that we have to take into account.' But international law considerations were not finding much support. CNN described how officials were probably assessing that 'the "strictly legal" should not be allowed to cancel out a legitimate and necessary course of action, even if international law provides no clear support for intervention on humanitarian grounds.' Then UN Secretary General Ban Ki-moon announced that UN inspectors would be withdrawn on 29 August, anticipating likely US airstrikes. As *The Guardian* described it, 'The accelerated departure of the UN weapons inspectors was reminiscent of a similar hasty exit from Iraq more than a decade ago, after receiving a tip-off from Western intelligence agencies that US air strikes against Saddam Hussein's regime were imminent.' The threat of military engagement was growing.

But the failure of earlier wars in the Middle East – Iraq, Afghanistan, Libya – continued to resonate. Sixty per cent of Americans remained opposed to US military intervention in Syria even if chemical weapons were involved. And quickly, anti-war organizations targeted Congress and the White House, building opposition to the drive toward war. The goal was to raise the political cost of US military intervention, and more members of Congress moved towards hesitation and then opposition to new military involvement.

Then the international conditions began to change. On 29 August, in a stunning blow to the government, the

British Parliament voted against Prime Minister David Cameron's request for authorization for a military strike on Syria. Cameron immediately announced: 'It is clear to me that the British Parliament, reflecting the views of the British people, does not want to see British military action. I get that, and the government will act accordingly.' It represented a major blow to the Obama administration's effort to establish an international coalition.

In response, President Obama changed his position. On 31 August, he appeared in the White House Rose Garden and announced: 'I have decided that the United States should take military action against Syrian regime targets... Our military has positioned assets in the region. The Chairman of the Joint Chiefs has informed me that we are prepared to strike whenever we choose. Moreover, the Chairman has indicated to me that our capacity to execute this mission is not time-sensitive; it will be effective tomorrow, or next week, or one month from now. And I'm prepared to give that order. But having made my decision as Commander-in-Chief based on what I am convinced is our national security interests, I'm also mindful that I'm the President of the world's oldest constitutional democracy. I've long believed that our power is rooted not just in our military might, but in our example as a government of the people, by the people, and for the people. And that's why I've made a second decision: I will seek authorization for the use of force from the American people's representatives in Congress.' It was a huge stand-down for the White House.

But Congress had yet to weigh in, and it was far from certain that it would stand up to the pro-war pressure from the White House, the media, and beyond. Anti-war campaigning escalated. Thousands, eventually hundreds of thousands, of letters, calls, visits, emails and petitions flooded the offices of members of the House and the Senate. Activists followed members in their home districts, seizing the microphones at town meetings to demand debate over the threat of war. It was an unprecedented mobilization aimed at preventing Congress from authorizing a seemingly imminent war. More and more members were signing on to letters and statements saying they would oppose military force, though it was difficult because alternatives were still not widely familiar enough to provide political safety for many members. Then it began to appear that there would not be the necessary 60 votes in the Senate supporting the use of force, and the possibility of a positive vote in the House of Representatives was looking less and less likely.

A week later, Russian President Vladimir Putin offered a solution. At a 9 September press conference a journalist asked US Secretary of State John Kerry whether there was anything that could prevent a US attack on Syria. He replied, seemingly off the cuff, that Syria could surrender its chemical weapons stockpile to the international community within a week. His Russian counterpart, foreign minister Sergei Lavrov, responded with an offer: 'If the establishment of international control over chemical weapons in that country would allow avoiding strikes, we will immediately start working with Damascus... We are calling on the Syrian leadership to not only agree on placing chemical weapons storage sites under international control, but also on its subsequent destruction and fully joining the treaty on prohibition of chemical weapons.' The Syrian government quickly agreed.

In response, the Senate majority leader announced that the war vote scheduled for 11 September would now be postponed. The Russian initiative to destroy Syria's chemical weapons quickly morphed into an international coalition. With US-Russian collaboration at its core, that multilateral disarmament alliance succeeded in identifying, removing and destroying Syria's entire known chemical arsenal by the middle of August 2014.

Neither the House of Representatives nor the US Senate ever voted on military strikes against Syria. The anti-war mobilizations – US and UK – had triumphed. For the moment...

Did the US start bombing Syria in August 2014 to save the Yazidis stranded on Mount Sinjar?

By the summer of 2014 virtually all US troops had been out of Iraq for two and a half years. The Middle East was still aflame, with the aftermath of the Libya assault, the collapse of the Arab Spring, especially in Egypt, and most of all the escalating multi-party Syrian civil war all causing new and greater violence. ISIS was gaining ground, seizing territory in what would soon become a huge swath of Syria and Iraq. In early June ISIS captured Mosul, Iraq's second-largest city, as Iraqi army units collapsed and fled, leaving their weapons behind.

On 19 June President Obama reassured a war-weary public: 'American forces will not be returning to combat in Iraq.' He added, though: 'but we will help Iraqis as they take the fight to terrorists who threaten the Iraqi people, the region, and American interests as well.' That caveat made clear that moves toward a new US war, again in Iraq and perhaps beyond, were coming closer.

The White House said it was 'only' sending 275 soldiers to protect the already heavily guarded US embassy in Baghdad. It was 'only' sending 300 Special Forces, and they were 'only' advisers. The Pentagon said there was 'only' one aircraft carrier in the region, and a few other warships. Missile strikes were 'only' being considered, and no ground troops would be sent. Given the US failure to bring security or stability, let alone democracy, to Iraq with 150,000 troops at a time cycling through multiple deployments in an eight-year war, it wasn't clear what a few hundred troops, warplanes and warships were supposed to accomplish.

But within two months the pressure mounted for

even greater military engagement. The immediate cause was a humanitarian crisis emerging on Mount Sinjar, a mountainous area west of Mosul in Iraq just over the Syrian border. The timing of the quite-sudden shift in US policy, in favour of an immediate military response to the horrific massacres, beheadings and such that had been under way for some time already, also served as a useful distraction from the growing momentum of global opposition to Israel's 50-day war on Gaza.

ISIS militants attacked the mostly Kurdish Yazidi town of Sinjar on 3 August, killing men and kidnapping women. Thousands fled the attack, seeking refuge on Mount Sinjar. There they found relative safety from the attacks, but conditions were dire. There were thousands of families, with many children, trapped on the mountain, facing the midsummer heat with virtually no water or food.

On 6 August, President Obama spoke from the White House Rose Garden. 'The US cannot and should not intervene every time there is a crisis in the world,' he said. But in the case of the Yazidis, he added, 'I believe the US cannot turn a blind eye.' Obama authorized the Pentagon to go, and US planes dropped food and water on 8 August.

Obama's authorization, however, went far beyond a humanitarian response – he used the same speech to call for direct military intervention against ISIS, starting with airstrikes in Iraq. 'I know that many of you are rightly concerned about any American military action in Iraq, even limited strikes like these,' he said. 'I understand that. I ran for this office in part to end our war in Iraq and welcome our troops home, and that's what we've done. As Commander-in-Chief, I will not allow the United States to be dragged into fighting another war in Iraq.'

But the President seemed to be limiting the definition of 'another war in Iraq' to a scenario of tens or hundreds of thousands of US ground troops being sent to fight. Other military engagement apparently did not meet his criteria for another war in Iraq. The mantra 'no boots on the ground' would continue to be heard, as if officially designated combat ground troops were the only force that equals war. President Obama's actual authorization called for targeted airstrikes not only to help the Yazidis stranded on Mount Sinjar but also to be used against ISIS forces thought to be moving toward Erbil, the capital of Iraq's semi-autonomous Kurdish region.

The authorization was explained as a response to the humanitarian crisis facing the Yazidis and protection of US citizens – the latter factor useful as an excuse for the Obama administration ignoring the need for congressional authorization to return to war in Iraq. It wasn't clear whether and which US citizens might be at risk; there were a few dozen US diplomats and perhaps 200 US troops in and around Erbil, as well as some Americans who lived and worked there, but there were no indications any of them had been particularly targeted. Some reports indicated that the US citizen justification was based on the notion that ISIS might try to destroy the Mosul dam, which could create major damage downriver, perhaps even in Baghdad – and there were 5,000 US diplomats, troops and military contractors staffing one of the largest US embassies in the world there. But again, there was no indication, not even any claim, that Americans had been singled out. President Obama's claim that the US was 'uniquely capable' of providing humanitarian assistance to the stranded Yazidis also turned out not to be true. The United Nations, even before Obama's 6 August statement, had offered to provide technical help to the Iraqi government to establish a humanitarian airdrop programme – something that would have avoided the militarization inevitable in any Pentagon-run programme. The Iraqi government had rejected the UN offer, claiming that the global organization did not have the technical capacity to carry it out. But instead of pressuring the US-backed government in Baghdad to take up the UN offer, perhaps agreeing to provide whatever support might have helped further boost United Nations capacity, the US ignored the UN and announced its own plan.

The US military had already experienced the problems inherent in linking humanitarian airdrops with bombing raids. The last time this happened was in Afghanistan in November 2001, when the US Air Force was dropping food packs wrapped in bright yellow plastic to make them easily spotted by Afghan refugees fleeing the US bombing of the cities. But at the same time the US was dropping cluster bombs also wrapped with the same bright yellow plastic. No-one knows how many children were killed running to pick up what they thought were food packages that turned out to be cluster bombs.

As it turned out, very little US airpower was used on or around Mount Sinjar – only about four sets of US airstrikes were launched at ISIS positions surrounding the mountain. Far more airstrikes were launched to protect Erbil. On Mount Sinjar itself, the Yazidis were saved not by the US military but by a Syrian Kurdish militia, known as the YPG, or People's Protection Units, which is the Syrian affiliate of the better-known PKK, or Kurdish Workers Party of Turkey. The PKK has long been on Washington's list of 'foreign terrorist organizations', so there was a great reluctance in the White House and the Pentagon to acknowledge the role the YPG played in opposing ISIS in Syria in general and in rescuing those stranded on Mount Sinjar in particular. The Yazidis trapped there were able to escape not primarily as a result of US airstrikes, but because the YPG was able to punch an opening through ISIS lines, establishing a protected corridor. They led thousands of Yazidi families down the mountain to safety over the border into Syria, and then along the border to a much safer area where they were able to cross back into Iraq.

The Mount Sinjar crisis provided the Obama administration with the political cover necessary to return to war in Iraq. Despite statements from White

House officials that the US was not there to act as the air force of the Kurds or of the Shi'a-dominated Iraqi government, that was exactly what was under way. As the *New York Times* put it: 'offensive strikes on militant targets around Erbil and Baghdad would take American involvement in the conflict to a new level – in effect, turning the American Air Force into the Iraqi Air Force.'

Who are the 'moderates' in Syria?

The term 'moderate' has come to be used in Syria to describe political and military forces – people and groups – who oppose the government of Bashar al-Assad, who are more or less secular rather than Islamist, and, crucially, who are more or less pro-Western. This is the basis of the US effort to vet or approve opposition forces who might receive US or allied assistance – military, financial, or political. It has little to do with local support or legitimacy.

In early 2015, the Pentagon announced some of the details of its long-delayed plan to train Syrian rebels, who would supposedly be prepared to focus their fight against ISIS and put aside their opposition to the Syrian regime of Bashar al-Assad. Planned to involve 5,400 would-be fighters to be trained in Turkey, Qatar and Saudi Arabia for a year or more, the plan amounted to an acknowledgement that the US-backed 'moderate' Syrian rebels that Washington had been talking about supporting for three or four years still did not exist as a genuine fighting force. Instead the US would try to create a whole new force.

The US faced enormous challenges in trying to identify, vet, arm and train a 'moderate' rebel army. As of September 2014, according to Syria scholar Joshua Landis:

> The US is arming and funding 12 to 14 militias in northern Syria and 60 more groups in the south, according to the head

of the Syrian Opposition Coalition. These militias have not, thus far, been particularly successful on the battlefield, and none has national reach. Most are based on one charismatic commander or a single region and have not articulated clear ideologies. All depend on foreign money.

The vast majority of Syria's rebel groups have been deemed too Islamist, too sectarian and too anti-democratic by the US – and these are the groups ranged against the ISIL. They span the Salafist ideological gamut, from al-Qaeda's Nusra Front to the 40,000-strong conglomeration of rebel forces united under the banner of the Islamic Front. Despite US skepticism, some of the Sunni Arab regimes Obama has courted as key allies in the anti-ISIL effort have worked with these groups.

Gulf countries reportedly poured money into the Islamic Front until the US convinced them to stop. Islamic Front leaders decried democracy as the 'dictatorship of the strong' and called for building an Islamic state. Zahran Alloush, the military chief of the Islamic Front, spooked Americans by insisting that Syria be 'cleansed of Shi'a and Alawites'...

Turkey insists that the US arm these anti-ISIL Islamist rebel groups, including the Nusra Front. Disagreement over which rebels to back is one of the reasons Ankara has refused the US requests to use Turkish territory to train rebel forces and as a base from which to carry out attacks on ISIL. The US's principal allies simply do not agree on which rebel forces are sufficiently moderate to qualify for support.

Last year the US tried to unite Western-friendly militias under a supreme military command, but that effort proved a debacle. In December the Islamic Front overran the supreme military command of the Free Syrian Army and ransacked its numerous warehouses and depots, making off with large stashes of US and Saudi supplies. The US-backed fighters were hogtied and left in their underwear. When US Ambassador Robert Ford requested that the Islamic Front return the stolen items, he received no response.

Along with its regional allies – Saudi Arabia, Qatar, Jordan, Turkey and the UAE – Washington began urging those disparate opposition forces deemed secular and pro-Western enough, although already divided into dozens of separate organizations and militias, to form a unified political movement for negotiations and a unified military command with whom the US and other governments could engage. The forms took shape – the National Coalition for Syrian Revolution and Opposition Forces, known as the Syrian National Coalition, was created in November 2012 and was quickly anointed with US legitimacy as the official political force, and the Free Syrian Army became the official recipient of money and weapons from the Gulf states, with talk of training from the US. But the lack of substance behind those forms remained a problem. By September 2015 the plan's colossal failure was clear. On 16 September General Lloyd Austin, chief of the US Central Command, admitted to Congress that of the planned 5,400, only 54 had actually been trained. And when members of Congress asked how many of those trained fighters remained in the fight, the general answered: 'it's a small number... we're talking four or five.'

Who are the key forces within the Syrian conflict?

The Syrian National Coalition was made up primarily of exiles – many of them longtime, brave opponents of the Assad regime, representing a wide range of politics, ideas and constituencies (and some represented no clear constituencies at all). Not surprisingly, they had a very difficult time agreeing on strategy, negotiating positions, what to call for from the US and the rest of the international community, or anything else. They bickered over leadership positions and spokespeople. And most important, they had few connections to, and even less accountability to, the internal opposition movement inside Syria. That movement included the remnants of the original nonviolent political opposition activists, those who had not been arrested, forced into exile, wounded or killed, many of whom still opposed the militarization of the popular movement, as well as the widely disparate political/military organizations that had emerged later. They made clear to the world, as individual organizations and to some degree collectively, that the Syrian National Coalition did not speak for or represent them. A key point of contention was on the question of negotiating with the regime – many internal opposition forces were willing to consider negotiations even if they were not based on the pre-condition of Assad being removed from power; most of the external leaders were not.

Then there was the Free Syrian Army (FSA). Based in Turkey and with its origins in the cohort of former Syrian soldiers who defected to the opposition with their weapons in the first months of the uprising, it seemed like the logical core of a unified rebel military. But soon after its creation in 2011 it expanded to include the wide array of militias and fighters, Islamist and secular, who agreed on little beyond a shared opposition to the Assad regime. By the middle of 2012, infighting within and between the various FSA groups had increased.

The credibility of the military opposition was soon compromised. Syrian refugees who had been driven out by the fighting expressed bitterness about the many officers and generals who had defected from the Syrian military and left the country. The refugees were angry that so many former soldiers chose to stay in Turkey, and they demanded that the experienced military officers return to Syria to assist the opposition fighters. At the same time, reports surfaced of the FSA and other opposition forces committing serious human rights violations and war crimes. According to the *Wall Street Journal*, 'aid groups told the State Department that [al-Qaeda-linked] Nusra didn't interfere with their humanitarian deliveries, while elements of the Free Syrian Army, which included trusted commanders, sometimes did.'

The practices of the Free Syrian Army were sometimes indistinguishable from some of the most extreme elements of the Islamist opposition. In September 2014, the FSA beheaded six captured ISIS prisoners – just days after the ISIS beheadings of two white Americans, journalists James Foley and Robert Sotloff. The brutality of the ISIS beheadings dominated mainstream media for days and was perhaps the single most important factor in turning US public opinion toward support for direct military re-engagement in Iraq. There was far less discussion of the FSA executions – the 'moderate' rebel group first killed an African-American apparently fighting with ISIS and then beheaded the six non-American ISIS fighters they had captured.

At the same time Islamist or jihadi organizations, some of them Syrian but many made up primarily of foreign fighters, began to appear in Syria, especially in the north – and they soon became far more powerful than the FSA organizations. The most influential was the Nusra Front, al-Qaeda's Syrian franchise, which imposed a harsh form of Islamic law on its fighters and on civilians even as it led key battles against the regime's army and made clear that its goals linked the overthrow of Assad's government with the establishment of sharia law in areas under their control. The FSA continued to lose power and influence to their Islamist 'allies' – and many FSA fighters abandoned their secular militias to join Nusra or later ISIS, seeing that the Islamist forces were better armed, paid better salaries, and were actually winning more victories.

That phenomenon expanded when ISIS appeared as a separate force in Syria in early 2013, following its split with Nusra (see 'How did ISIS begin to expand beyond Iraq?'). During those first months ISIS fought its Islamist and secular opposition rivals far more than it fought the Syrian regime's military. And ISIS continued to expand. *Al-Monitor* reported in November 2013 that 'ISIS opened the door for new members without checking the quality of the new members. ISIS started paying $200 a month for each fighter, and thousands of men in ISIS's area of control joined the group.'

The rising power of the Islamists and relative weakening of the secular FSA-linked forces may have contributed to the US announcing its intention to provide $123 million in aid to the Free Syrian Army in April 2013. But that aid was officially limited to 'non-lethal' assistance, usually consisting of uniforms, food and medicine, sometimes military gear such as night-vision goggles, but explicitly not weapons. Given the divisions and tensions within and between the various components of the FSA, it is unclear whether more weapons at that time would have changed the military situation on the ground, but, either way, the FSA continued to deteriorate and it continued to lose fighters to the Nusra Front and other Islamist groups. From some time in 2012 the CIA was already engaged in training 'vetted' rebel fighters in Jordan, but it was a small-scale (and officially covert) operation, and there has been little evidence of an impact on the battlefield.

While many secular fighters joined ISIS, in other areas the so-called moderates fought alongside ISIS, often openly recognizing that they shared the goal of overthrowing the Syrian government. By late 2014 the US priority had explicitly shifted to attacking ISIS, with the Syrian regime a secondary or even tertiary target, but for the vast majority of opposition fighters – including those deemed 'moderate', secular, pro-Western – the target remained the Assad regime. And whatever the priorities of the US, most of those 'moderates' were prepared to work with anyone to achieve that goal.

But in fact the US did not believe that success was ever possible. As far back as 2013, Patrick Cockburn described how 'the US and its allies have responded to the rise of ISIS by descending into fantasy. They pretend they are fostering a "third force" of moderate Syrian rebels to fight both Assad and ISIS, though in private

Western diplomats admit this group doesn't really exist outside a few beleaguered pockets.' That view was even shared by some military leaders of the Free Syrian Army itself. In September 2014 an FSA commander told the *Washington Post* that Washington's effort to link the various FSA units into a unified military force was 'a cut and paste of previous FSA failures'.

In August 2014 President Obama told the *New York Times* the idea that arming the Syrian rebels would have made a difference has 'always been a fantasy. This idea that we could provide some light arms or even more sophisticated arms to what was essentially an opposition made up of former doctors, farmers, pharmacists and so forth, and that they were going to be able to battle not only a well-armed state but also a well-armed state backed by Russia, backed by Iran, a battle-hardened Hizbullah, that was never in the cards.'

In the cards or not, in September 2014 a new coalition of 'moderate' militia groups was announced in Turkey, linking the Supreme Military Council of Syria, which included the FSA, as well as the predominantly Christian Syriac Military Council. Created under the auspices of several members of the US Congress and the staff of the US House Foreign Affairs Committee, the coalition's goal was ostensibly to organize a unified military fight against both the Assad government and ISIS. But, as CNN reported after the meeting: 'While the Supreme Military Council of Syria includes the Free Syrian Army, which is considered one of the leading moderate forces, there are questions about other members of the alliance. The Syrian Revolutionary Front reportedly signed a deal with ISIS in one suburb in Damascus, and another – the Hazzam group – put out a statement this week condemning US airstrikes.'

Syria expert Joshua Landis assessed that a victory by the US-backed opposition would be very dangerous. 'The FSA wouldn't bring unified rule in Syria, they would bring Somalia,' he said.

Wasn't the original Syrian opposition a nonviolent movement? What happened to it?

The original democratic opposition was initially nonviolent, and elements of this movement remain intact, although seriously weakened by the violence engulfing the country. As long-time ABC News Middle East chief Charles Glass described it:

> the other opposition, the people who actually started this, people who had done time in prison over the years, who were prisoners of the Assad regime who wanted popular demonstrations, who wanted civil disobedience, who wanted negotiations with the regime, to have a transition – a peaceful transition – in which there would ultimately be free elections by which the regime could, would lose, those people's voices are being drowned out in the cacophony of artillery and rifle fire all around Syria at this time. These people, I think they are disenchanted with the US. ...[T]hose people in the peaceful opposition do not want to become pawns in a superpower game.

There are strategic costs paid by those who advocate taking up arms against regimes. Some opposition activists may have held a moral or other kind of commitment to nonviolence. But for many more, the rejection of armed struggle, even in circumstances of horrific civilian casualties, was based on the recognition that once a nonviolent protest movement turns to arms, it loses not only its moral legitimacy in the eyes of many but, more importantly, loses its mass character. And it is the continuation of the mass, popular involvement of huge proportions that creates an engaged, mobilized population willing and prepared to defend the democratic gains of these revolutionary processes whenever they may be won.

Opposition activist Haytham Manna described how in Syria:

the first negative result of the use of arms was to undermine the broad popular support necessary to transform the uprising into a democratic revolution. It made the integration of competing demands – rural v urban, secular v Islamist, old opposition v revolutionary youth – much more difficult. The resort to arms gave birth to fragmented groups that have no political programme. Turkey trained army dissidents on its territory, and a group of them announced the birth of the Free Syrian Army under the supervision of Turkish military intelligence. Most militants inside Syria now carry a 'Free Army' logo, but beyond a name there is no co-ordination or organized political harmony.

In any political struggle, when mass mobilization is replaced by small groups waging military battles, non-participants in the armed struggle become victims, often of the violence from their 'own' side. This is most glaring in situations of full-scale civil war, as in Syria.

One of the most influential coalitions of indigenous Syrian political activists is the Local Coordination Committees – Syria (LCC), which came together in mid-2011 in the first months of the uprising. Uniting separate committees and organizations from a number of Syrian cities, by early 2015 their website listed 14 local and regional groups – from Dara and Homs to the Syrian coast, Damascus and Damascus suburbs, and even Raqqa, the self-declared 'capital' of ISIS.

In August 2011, when the first calls for US and other foreign military intervention were coming from Syrians inside and outside the country, the LCC issued the following statement:

In an unprecedented move over the past several days, Syrians in Syria and abroad have been calling for Syrians to take up arms, or for international military intervention. This call comes after five and a half months of the Syrian regime's systematic abuse of the Syrian people, whereby tens of thousands of peaceful protesters have been detained and tortured, and more than 2,500 killed. The regime has given every indication that it will continue its brutal approach, while the majority of Syrians feel they are unprotected in their own homeland in the face of the regime's crimes.

While we understand the motivation to take up arms or call for military intervention, we specifically reject this position as we find it unacceptable politically, nationally and ethically. Militarizing the revolution would minimize popular support and participation in the revolution. Moreover, militarization would undermine the gravity of the humanitarian catastrophe involved in a confrontation with the regime. Militarization would put the Revolution in an arena where the regime has a distinct advantage, and would erode the moral superiority that has characterized the Revolution since its beginning.

Our Palestinian brothers are experienced in leading by example. They gained the support of the entire Palestinian community, as well as world sympathy, during the first Intifada ('stones'). The second Intifada, which was militarized, lost public sympathy and participation. It is important to note that the Syrian regime and Israeli enemy used identical measures in the face of the two uprisings.

The objective of Syria's Revolution is not limited to over-throwing the regime. The Revolution also seeks to build a democratic system and national infrastructure that safeguards the freedom and dignity of the Syrian people. Moreover, the Revolution is intended to ensure independence and unity of Syria, its people, and its society.

We believe that the overthrow of the regime is the initial goal of the Revolution, but it is not an end in itself. The end goal is freedom for Syria and all Syrians. The method by which the regime is overthrown is an indication of what Syria will be like post-regime. If we maintain our peaceful demonstrations – which include our cities, towns and villages; and our men, women, and children – the possibility of democracy in our country is much greater. If an armed confrontation or international military intervention becomes a reality, it will be virtually impossible to establish a legitimate foundation for a proud future Syria.

The LCC maintained their commitment to nonviolence but also participated in the broader Syrian National Council (SNC), which included both nonviolent political activists and those supporting the Free Syrian Army. The SNC is made up of a relatively wide range of reformist intellectuals, the Muslim Brotherhood and many individual activists representing youth, Assyrian and Kurdish movements. The SNC has been willing to consider negotiations with the Syrian regime, but has mainly insisted that such talks focus on power transitions.

That was distinct from the position of the National Coordinating Committee (NCC), a bloc of primarily left and Kurdish parties inside Syria. Created around the same time as the Syrian National Council, the NCC also maintained a commitment to nonviolence but was willing to negotiate with the regime without preconditions.

Numerous other grassroots organizations and coalitions were created as well, including those focused on mobilizing nonviolent protests, media activism, providing humanitarian assistance especially to besieged communities, and documenting human rights violations. US and international attention largely ignored their work, choosing to engage instead with those political opposition groups supporting US and Western military intervention, and tied to the Free Syrian Army.

The work of the grassroots continued in the face of enormous challenges. Not surprisingly, even the commitment to nonviolence came under question. Two years after its statement that if 'international military intervention becomes a reality, it will be virtually impossible to establish a legitimate foundation for a proud future Syria', the LCC faced the US threat to bomb Syria in retaliation for the chemical weapon attack of August 2013.

In a statement showing how complex the considerations were, the LCC responded with a nuanced statement that made clear the activists were not endorsing a US military strike, but were setting conditions that any such strike would have to follow if it was to achieve anything of value for Syrians.

The Syrian people have never welcomed a foreign military intervention, but as it faced the oppression, it was forced to revolt ... Today, the signs are indicating a serious possibility of an American strike against the regime that would merely defend the Red Line of the use of chemical weapons, which Assad has repeatedly challenged. Apparently, the main concern of the West in this regard is based on international balance and interests, not on the serious attempt to rescue a people who are striving for freedom and dignity, and dying for that, every day.

A limited strike to merely warn Assad will lead to nothing but increase in his violence, as well as to his complete confidence that no one would prevent him from killing. Such a transient strike will only become an international community approval of his use of non-chemical weaponry, if it really succeeds in preventing future use of chemical. In the end no one will pay the price but the Syrian people.

It is a difficult moment and a turning point in the history of Syrians, it requires a high sense of responsibility, from us, and from the entire world, as well as wisdom, not hesitation and egoism.

Any strike to the regime must aim to paralyze, with attention and precision, its Air Forces, artillery and missiles arsenal, being used continuously against civilian areas, with an impact not far from that of Mass Destruction weapons. A strike must also prioritize civilians and their safety, rather than being at their cost. Moreover, it needs to be accompanied by close co-ordination with, and sufficient support to the Syrian opposition, both political and armed; in order to allow for better organization and progress. Such an empowerment is crucial, as it enables hope in the hearts of Syrians, whose despair and agony are the basis for extremism.

As opposers, revolutionaries and activists, it is our

responsibility to stand side by side today, in order to clarify our national interests and humanitarian necessities, to tell the entire world that abandoning a people equals abandoning humanity itself, and that an intervention in Syria must be in favor of the Syrians' needs and voices, respecting them as well as their future's sovereignty.

The weakening of the nonviolent political opposition continued. In early 2013 the noted Syrian writer and human rights activist Haytham Manna described the contradiction. On the one hand he continued to assert the following: 'In modern history, no state exists where gnarled violence gave rise to a democratic system... and we do not have a single case of a military victory in a similar situation that did not carry viruses of the spectrum of extremism, eradication and revenge. We have warned and continue to warn of the repercussions of violence on social cohesion and civil peace, and the unity of Syria. It is clearly visible that the project of political violence does not represent an expression of class status, or national demands or democratic aspirations. Political violence in Syria is pushing a thoughtful and deliberate social mobility towards sectarianism and factionalism and extremism as a custodian of death, murder and revenge.'

But at the same time he recognized that for some even within his own organization, nonviolent political mobilization had 'shifted from being seen as high principles to being an accusation, and the three nos that were adopted by the National Co-ordination Body (no to violence, no to sectarianism, no to foreign intervention) were marked out as complicity and weakness in the face of dictatorial power.'

In June that year *The Economist* described a meeting with two members of the NCC, both of whom had spent a decade or more imprisoned by the Assad regime. They said they wanted to see the fall of the regime, 'but that the arming of the revolution has taken it down "the wrong path".' 'We are against all arms,' says Safwan Akash, a member from Hama. 'That was the biggest mistake in the revolution.' But supporters of the nonviolent political movement did not then have an alternative strategy to move forward.

By early 2014 the Lebanese magazine *al Akhbar* was asking the headline question: 'Where are Syria's nonviolent revolutionaries today?' As the armed groups took over the initiative of the anti-Assad uprising, many of the nonviolent protesters refused to join the military struggle. *Al Akhbar* notes: 'Some preferred to leave the country in order to escape the new reality where the nonviolent protest movement was in decline... Those whose circumstances did not allow them to leave, are living today the worst days of their lives. Some of them have persisted in their activism in non-governmental civil society organizations, whose numbers have increased during the events in Syria, or in the Coordinating Committees on social networking sites.'

But they face extraordinary challenges, including repression and the threat of arrest or worse from the Syrian security forces or various armed groups, as well as the problems facing all Syrian civilians caught up in the midst of a brutal civil war. *Al Akhbar* quotes one young activist who blames the regime's response to the original protests, and adds, 'We were a group of patriotic men and women participating in the protests and spreading the values of national unity. After the revolution became militarized, we had no role to play. The fighting destroyed the civil movement.'

As Patrick Cockburn reminds us in *The Jihadis Return*, 'revolutions are notorious for devouring their earliest and most humane advocates, but few have done so with the speed and ferocity of Syria's.' The little bit of good news is that the original, democratic, largely nonviolent Syrian movement that rose in early 2011 as part of the Arab Spring has not entirely disappeared. But as the multi-sided civil war continues to devastate Syria, reclaiming the movement's role as the centre of the country's political motion remains a project for the future.

How successful has US involvement in the Syrian war been?

A *Wall Street Journal* report in late January 2015 analysed one of the signature strategies of the US war: the campaign to arm and train so-called moderate forces in Syria. Although the US priority had shifted in Syria from regime change to getting rid of ISIS, the role of the anti-Assad rebels vetted and approved (in some cases first mobilized) by the US remained key. It was not an optimistic view.

> All sides now agree that the US's effort to aid moderate fighters battling the Assad regime has gone badly. The CIA program was the riskiest foray into Syria since civil war erupted in 2011. Syrian President Bashar al-Assad is clinging to power after more than 200,000 deaths blamed on the war. Moderate fighters control only a fraction of northern Syria, while Islamic State and al-Qaeda's official affiliate, the Nusra Front, have gained ground. Last fall, Nusra overran one trusted commander and seized another's equipment.
>
> Entire CIA-backed rebel units, including fighters numbering in the 'low hundreds' who went through the training program, have changed sides by joining forces with Islamist brigades, quit the fight or gone missing....
>
> Some Obama administration officials say the covert effort accomplished about as much as it could considering the chaotic circumstances in northern Syria and policy disagreements in Washington and elsewhere.

So little was accomplished, not only because of chaos in Syria and policy fights in Washington, but also because of the reliance on military actions in situations where no military solution was possible. The administration was guaranteed to fail.

So much of what was – and still is – needed to respond to the catastrophe of the Syrian civil war and the rise of ISIS across the region has been ignored, sidelined or simply done badly.

- There was no serious (meaning equivalent to that invested in the military campaign) effort by the administration to create new diplomatic initiatives with Iran and Russia through the investment of money, presidential attention, the assignment of top diplomats or other measures.

- There was insufficient continuing work to recognize the centrality of the United Nations in establishing a new forum for regional and global diplomacy aimed at ending the Syrian war.

- The Obama administration did not sufficiently support the UN effort, begun in 2014, to create local ceasefires in Syria designed to provide immediate humanitarian assistance to besieged communities and potentially to achieve broader ceasefire goals in the future.

- The US never showed enough support for initiatives by other countries or civil-society initiatives to bring opposing sides together for negotiations. The US provided insufficient financial support for humanitarian assistance to the burgeoning numbers of refugees and internally displaced people, while spending billions on military escalation.

- The US has not acknowledged that its foreign policy not only antagonizes people across the region but in many cases also leads to support for even the most extreme terrorist organizations. The most prominent of these antagonizing policies have been: the invasion and occupation of Iraq; the war on terror's rendition, detention, interrogation and torture policies; and the uncritical economic, political and diplomatic backing and protection of Israel's occupation and apartheid policies.

- The Obama administration has only a limited understanding of how the war on terror relied on anti-Arab racism and Islamophobia to shape a militarized, surveillance-based response to terrorism. This approach not only violated the US Constitution and international human rights laws, and imposed collective punishments on entire targeted communities, but was also guaranteed to fail. And the limited recognition of the problem never led to alternative policies being proposed.

- The US claimed that diplomatic, humanitarian and other strategies were necessary alongside the military action, but the Obama administration never seriously pursued those other goals, and in fact the military attacks made the other work far more difficult.
- The US military responses to the Syrian civil war and the rise of ISIS have made the situation worse, not better. Whatever else the US has learned from more than 10 years of US intervention in Iraq, it should be eminently clear that it is not possible to defeat Islamist extremists with airstrikes.

5 The Arab Spring

What was the Arab Spring all about?

The democratic movements that spread from Tunisia in 2010 on to Egypt early in 2011, then to Bahrain and Libya, Yemen and Syria, and beyond, quickly became known collectively as the Arab Spring. Each had its own national particularities, but there were enough parallels and enough shared influence between them to legitimize a regional description. The uprisings began, in each case, as nonviolent civil-society protests against government repression, human rights violations, economic injustice. The demands varied somewhat, for bread or jobs, for the right to speak or the end of dictatorship, but at their core these were demands for the rights of citizenship, for dignity.

It was a set of uprisings that showed a level of revolutionary fervour not visible in the Middle East in perhaps a generation – and that meant that the legacy of US-dominated governments across the region would never be the same. It did not, however, mean that all – indeed any – of these revolutionary processes were actually revolutions. They were – and remain – transformative social movements, to varying degrees crossing fault-lines of class, religion, sect, gender. But they were not one-off events, in which the ousting of a dictator or the resignation of a hated autocrat and the calling for new elections necessarily meant the immediate announcement of a whole new society.

There was never going to be a direct, nonstop trajectory toward the victory of democracy, equality, dignity – demands that were on so many protesters' lips. There would always be backward motion – even major disasters seeming to grow out of the initial protests. It was in that second phase – the defeats and reversals following the first heady mobilizations – that the first popularly elected president in Egypt was deposed in a coup followed by a long period of repression, that Libya collapsed into militarized anarchy, that Syria's escalating civil war led to the death of over 220,000 people, that ISIS emerged in the chaos, and that the US returned its troops and planes to the region in a new iteration of the global war on terror.

But it is much too early to give up on the Arab Spring's promise – that civil engagement, the creation of broad social movements and massive protest can indeed lead to new popular understandings of the rights of citizens, of human rights, of dignity. And those movements continue to influence public discourse and public action. The ability of mass mobilization in the street to cause friction and eventually division within the state apparatus – even within the military, police, and other agencies of repression – remains a newly recognized reality in the Arab world.

In Egypt, perhaps the most astonishing example of the Arab Spring's promise and its failures is the recognition that mobilized people in the streets led to the overthrow of a powerful, US-backed dictator. This certainly empowered the Egyptian public. It also set the stage for the military coup against the democratically elected President Mohamed Morsi, who had made numerous mistakes during his chaotic one-year reign, and who many activists thought could be turned out and replaced by the people themselves now empowered by their mobilization. Instead, it led to widespread popular support for a military coup, quickly backed by the US and US allies across the region, that imprisoned Morsi, killed more than a thousand peaceful protesters and arrested tens of thousands more, attacked journalists and human rights defenders, and installed a general as the new military president. But even after years of the new military dictatorship and repression, Egyptians continue to recognize, to hold on to, their right to have a say in their government – to claim the rights of citizens. It may be still more years ahead, but the Arab Spring is not a process that is over.

The challenges, however, remain formidable. Libya's collapse into armed chaos and Syria's descent into civil war represent the most dangerous iterations of this second phase of the Arab Spring. Human rights activists in Bahrain remain in jeopardy, with many imprisoned and facing torture as the regime continues to suppress the democratic movement that rose in 2011. Yemen's uprising accomplished the negotiated standing down of a US-backed autocrat in 2012. Yet, three years later, the country collapsed into civil war as Houthi rebels seized the capital and several other cities and forced the replacement president to flee the country, while Saudi Arabia led an anti-Houthi air assault that killed hundreds of civilians. Reclaiming popular mobilization and rebuilding social movements is going to be a very long-term project across the region.

It is also important to recognize the breadth of public support and involvement in the Arab Spring uprisings. In the US, the television coverage – one must single out the then-newly influential *Al Jazeera English* here – of the Tahrir Square mobilizations in Egypt accomplished a great deal in the struggle against anti-Arab racism and Islamophobia. Here were Egyptians – Arabs – speaking in their own voice, articulating their own demands, their own narrative. And they spoke English! And wore blue jeans and were on Facebook and had cellphones clamped to their ears! They were 'just like us'.

Except the vast majority of Egyptians don't speak English, don't use Facebook because they can't afford computers or internet access, and are not 'just like us'. Certainly the young, English-speaking tech-savvy activists who used social media to mobilize people and who soon became familiar to Western television watchers and social media fans played a huge role in Egypt's uprising. But the Tahrir Square protests that led to the ousting of the US-backed dictator Hosni Mubarak did not begin on Facebook in 2011.

The movement originated with the labour protests

of 2004, which led to huge strikes by textile workers in 2006. The mobilization of Egypt's workers, much of it outside the state-controlled official unions, played a huge role. The broader anti-dictatorship, democratic demands also had roots much earlier than the Facebook rebels of 2011, although many of the individual activists were part of both. In February 2003, Egyptian activists mobilized as part of the global protests against the then-looming US war in Iraq. Amazed by the millions of people pouring into the streets around the world, and embarrassed that they were unable to bring out many people in Cairo, they decided to work to build a movement for democracy – 'to do better', as one of them explains in *We Are Many*, a film about the global protests. 'Better' came in 2011 and resulted in the overthrow of a dictator. And the Muslim Brotherhood, the oldest Islamist organization in today's Arab world, eventually moved out of the shadowy sort-of-legal, sort-of-not position it had long held, to take its place at the centre of the protests.

The point is not to underestimate the importance of the mainly young, urban, secular activists who led important components of the Arab Spring uprising in Egypt and elsewhere. Rather it is to recognize that the mobilizations gained their power from their inclusion of workers, rural residents and older people as well, and the leadership these individuals brought. Many were not secular, but were motivated at least partly by their faith. Most Egyptian workers who participated in the labour strikes would not define themselves as secular. During the Arab Spring, mosques became crucial centres of information sharing, particularly when the regime shut down social-media sites and sometimes the entire internet at various points. Religious services in Tahrir Square rotated between Muslim prayers guarded by Coptic Christian activists and Christian services where Muslims kept watch, which presented an inter-religious, but not secular, identity for the protesters.

The protests in Tunisia evolved in similar fashion.

From the start, workers and middle-class professionals were involved, but the core of the demonstrators came from the disenchanted, disempowered, unemployed youth. Unlike in Egypt, they were often educated. Coming to symbolize their plight was Mohammed Bouazizi, the young man in the impoverished town of Sidi Bouzid who set himself ablaze to protest not only the unemployment and poverty, but also the humiliation and degradation he faced. His act sparked the actions that became the Arab Spring.

Unquestionably some of the challenges to the Arab Spring uprisings came from the protesters' decision in some countries to take up arms. There is a strategic cost paid for such a decision – even in circumstances of horrific civilian casualties, once a nonviolent protest movement turns to arms, it loses not only its moral legitimacy in the eyes of some, but also its mass character. And it is that mass, popular involvement of huge proportions of the population that makes possible victories against repressive regimes (Egypt, Tunisia) as well as creates the potential for an engaged, mobilized population willing and prepared to defend the democratic gains of these revolutionary processes.

Similarly, the call for outside military intervention, however understandable in the face of terrible regime violence, risks losing independence to foreign sponsors. Opposition to the calls for such intervention is often grounded less in abstract principles than in a pragmatic recognition that an independent, mass-based popular movement has the best chance of strategic victory, both in overthrowing a dictator and in reclaiming civil society for a once-dispossessed population. Unfortunately, in Syria the devastating effect of the regime's attacks over several years, along with the escalation of military attacks by the opposition beginning in mid-2011, created a kind of desperation. This meant more people were willing to support anything – including international military involvement – that they hoped might, just might, hold some possibility of improving conditions. But unfortunately conditions didn't improve, and the countries were suddenly flooded with arms and even fighters from outside, and the violence escalated.

As Seamus Milne wrote about the Syrian rebels in *The Guardian* in August 2012:

> the rapidly mushrooming dependence of their uprising on foreign support is a disaster – even more than was the case in Libya. After all, it is now officials of the dictatorial and sectarian Saudi regime who choose which armed groups get funding, not Syrians. And it is intelligence officials from the US, which sponsors the Israeli occupation of Syrian territory and dictatorships across the region, who decide which rebel units get weapons. Opposition activists insist they can maintain their autonomy, based on deep-rooted popular support. But the dynamic of external backing clearly risks turning groups dependent on it into instruments of their sponsors, rather than the people they seek to represent.

When the Arab Spring emerged as a regional phenomenon, the Obama administration seemed initially open to accepting the new reality of collapsing dictators and emerging more-or-less Islamist-oriented democracies in some parts of the Arab world the US had long dominated. Not everywhere, of course. The US would almost certainly not have even considered accepting such a new reality in Saudi Arabia, where oil influence and weapons sales were at stake. And by supporting the Saudi military intervention to quell the 2011 Pearl Roundabout protest movement in Bahrain, Washington served notice it had no intention of supporting democratization in a country whose absolute monarchs host the US Navy's Fifth Fleet – something that a democratic government in Bahrain just might have reconsidered. But even as the US hesitated on whether to urge Mubarak to step down in Egypt, how to engage with Morsi and thus with the Muslim Brotherhood, there was still some evidence of a shift away from the position that US influence could be maintained only by backing dictators across the region. The US was not about to abandon its commitment to regional hegemony in the Middle East, but the Arab Spring did seem to make possible a different relationship with popular Islamist forces – at least those deemed 'moderate' in US counter-terrorism jargon.

It was never certain, and Washington's rhetoric waffled. Before Mubarak stepped down Obama expressed cautious support for 'a government that is responsive to the aspirations of the Egyptian people'. Then-Secretary of State Clinton called for 'change that will respond to the legitimate grievances of the Egyptian people which the protests are all about'. But both stressed the need for an 'orderly' transition – something quite the opposite of popular uprisings like Tahrir Square. And Clinton pulled back from anything that might even hint of an opening to Islamist forces, explicitly rejecting, in a clear reference to the Muslim Brotherhood, 'any transition to a new government where oppression... would take root'. The crises of post-Arab Spring Egypt, Libya, Yemen and especially Syria allowed the US to pull back from its tentative gesture of openness toward popular democracy and Islamism.

The origin of ISIS, it should be noted, goes back significantly before the Arab Spring erupted, to the US occupation of Iraq. It is true that the Arab Spring's victories for dignity and democracy also set the stage for the current period of conflict and violence across the region. The chaos of Syria's civil war; the spread of weapons across Libya's borders into the rest of the region; an escalating civil war in Yemen; the return of military dictatorship to Egypt: all of these are huge setbacks. But they do not mean the Arab Spring has been permanently defeated.

Why did the US and NATO launch an air war in Libya to overthrow Qadafi?

Like other countries' versions of the Arab Spring, the Libyan uprising against the government of Muammar Qadafi began in February 2011 as a popular uprising protesting government repression, discrimination and lack of democracy. The protests began around the same time as those earlier ones in Tunisia and Egypt, and followed an initially similar trajectory. As with Tunis and Cairo, the roots of Libya's opposition extend further back.

What was different in Libya from those earlier iterations of the democratic revolutionary processes that swept the Arab world throughout that period was that in Libya, the opposition quickly ousted the regime from major cities. In much of eastern Libya, large sectors of the military was defecting to the opposition. Despite that, the Qadafi regime continued to attack opposition strongholds in the key eastern city of Benghazi and beyond, and very quickly Libyan activists moved to take up arms, joining with the defecting military units. Unlike Egypt and Tunisia, the other Arab states in which democratic upheavals were already under way, Libya moved quickly toward a direct military confrontation, much closer to a civil war.

The UN Security Council passed its first resolution on the Libya crisis on 26 February 2011, freezing assets, restricting the travel of Qadafi and his inner circle, and sending the issue to the International Criminal Court for investigation. The fighting continued, and on 17 March the Security Council passed another resolution, 1973, which formed the legal basis for military intervention in the Libyan civil war. It demanded 'an immediate ceasefire' and authorized establishment of a no-fly zone and the use of 'all means necessary' short of foreign occupation to protect civilians. But, when implemented, the resolution quickly resulted in a full-scale air war with the goal of overthrowing Qadafi – full-blown regime change was under way. (See 'What role is the United Nations playing...' below for more on UN decision-making on Libya.)

Many of Libya's armed protesters, though certainly not all, explicitly rejected international intervention, and were still able to consolidate significant levels of control of towns and cities, first in the east and quite quickly in the west. Reports from the western city of Misurata, not far from the capital of Tripoli, indicated that protesters backed by defecting army units were in control of the city from 21 February on. The *Financial Times* quoted a local worker in Misurata describing how 'the people are now organizing themselves into committees. Some are managing traffic, others are cleaning up after the fighting and the fires of previous days. There are also people handing out water and milk to the population.' It looked, for a brief time, very much like the self-organization of protesters in Tahrir Square in Egypt, in the short-lived Pearl Roundabout protests in Bahrain – and very much like the nonviolent, society-wide mobilization of the first Palestinian intifada of 1987-93.

The regime itself was quickly splintering, with high-ranking ministers and other officials resigning. The interior minister announced his support for what he called the 'February 17 Revolution' and urged the military to support the Libyan people's 'legitimate demands'. Libyan diplomats around the world, including the ambassadors to the US, Indonesia, Australia, India, Bangladesh and elsewhere, as well as virtually the entire staff of the Libyan mission to the United Nations, all resigned in protest at the regime's violence. The regime was collapsing.

But somehow, despite the fact that opposition forces were claiming real victories against the Libyan military, allegations took hold in capitals and in the press around the world that Qadafi's undoubted brutality meant that genocide was both inevitable and imminent. On the eighth anniversary of the US 'shock and awe' assault against Iraq, 19 March, airstrikes against Libya began. The first were by French warplanes that attacked Libyan government tanks in the desert outside of Benghazi – tanks which had been driven out of the city by rebel forces. Despite that evidence that the opposition was not facing imminent genocide and was in fact able to drive the regime's army out of the city, the ostensibly limited no-fly-zone resolution was quickly interpreted to justify full-scale air war.

Months of war followed, with the rapid collapse of the always-fragile structures of the Libyan state. In early April the armed opposition offered a ceasefire; neither the UN nor NATO used that offer to re-engage with the Libyan government in new negotiations. On 27 June the International Criminal Court issued arrest warrants for Qadafi and other officials on charges of crimes against humanity, and in September the United Nations lifted sanctions on the country and accepted the opposition's Transitional National Council as the legitimate government of Libya. Fighting continued, sporadically, and Qadafi was found and killed by opposition forces in October. Three days later, the opposition TNC declared victory and the end of the war.

What was the impact of the regime change in Libya?

The real consequences of the destruction of the Libyan state began to become apparent once the war officially ended, first with widespread instability inside the country, then with the massive flow of weapons out of Qadafi's storage facilities and out across Libya's borders to fuel unrest in central and north Africa and across the already roiling Middle East.

Then the other major consequence – anticipated or not by those who so quickly embraced regime change – erupted across Libya: the rise of extremist forces,

Islamist and otherwise, as the state institutions collapsed. Soon there were two separate rival parliaments, sitting a thousand kilometres apart, each claiming to be ruling post-Qadafi Libya. A UAE newspaper described the scene in October 2014:

> Trucks fitted with anti-aircraft cannon, troops and cement roadblocks protect the five-star hotel in Tobruk that is now the surreal last bastion of Libya's fugitive parliament.
>
> Holed up in the Dar Al Salam seaside resort and pretending that all is normal, elected legislators debate laws and plan the future from the eastern city where they fled last month after losing control of Tripoli and much of the country.
>
> A thousand kilometres away in the capital, a rival parliament sits, shunned by the international community and made up of members of an earlier assembly whose mandate has expired. It is making its own decisions, taking over ministries and staking a competing claim to rule the country.
>
> Four years after NATO missiles helped overthrow Muammar Qadafi, Libya is effectively divided, with two governments and two parliaments, each backed by rival militias.

And the two parliaments are backed not only by rival militias but by rival sets of international actors as well. The newer Tobruk parliament represents more or less secular, mostly Western-oriented Libyans, many of whom had spent years in exile and only returned after the overthrow of Qadafi. It has defined itself largely as being 'anti-Islamist', and its backing includes the militia of a US-trained Libyan general, Khalifa Hafter, who commanded part of Qadafi's army before being arrested for trying to overthrow the regime. He was released in a US-brokered deal, became a US citizen, and lived in the US for 20 years. The Tobruk parliament is backed by Saudi Arabia, Egypt and the UAE in the region – as well as by the US and its European allies. The originally elected parliament, whose mandate has since expired, sits in the original capital of Tripoli and includes a number of

Islamist forces grouped into a coalition known as Libya Dawn. It has some international backing from Qatar and Turkey.

Writing in *al-Araby*, analyst Vijay Prashad described how 'The NATO bombing of 2011 destroyed the state – the painfully thin institutions that held together this archipelago of cities. Out of the ashes of the Gadafi regime emerged a NATO-authorized government that had more interest in central banks and oil contracts than the creation of a new Libya. The West and its allies were not interested in the surrender of the old regime, no interest in creating a platform of reconciliation and patriotism. Various armed groups thrived as Western-backed liberals found themselves with little popular support and no real institutions to do their bidding. It is what sent Libya spiralling into chaos.'

During that chaos some Libyans travelled to Syria and Iraq to fight, joining jihadi forces in the civil wars and chaos there. Inside Libya, the post-Qadafi civil war pushed some of the Islamist forces toward far more extreme positions, some of them joining with Ansar al-Shariah, an earlier extremist group formed in Benghazi after the US-NATO bombing campaign. By 2014, some of the Libyans who had gone to fight in Syria or Iraq and who had seen, or even participated in the rise of ISIS, began returning to Libya. Some of them began calling themselves ISIS as well. In early 2015 the group took responsibility for rounding up and killing 21 Egyptian Coptic Christian labourers who had come to Libya to find work.

In mid-April 2015, foreign ministers of the US and several of its European allies issued a statement welcoming a new UN effort to organize a political unification process. They called on 'all participants to the dialogue to negotiate in good faith and use this opportunity to finalize agreements on the formation of a National Unity Government and make arrangements for an unconditional ceasefire.' In a presumably unintentional bit of irony, the governments responsible for the air war that created the chaos in Libya noted that 'in particular, we call for the immediate cessation of airstrikes and ground offensives. Such provocations undermine the UN talks and threaten chances for reconciliation.'

But in the meantime, the weapons set loose from Libyan arsenals during the earlier anti-Qadafi uprising and the US-NATO air strikes continue to fuel escalations as new crises erupt throughout an expanding region: in Mali and elsewhere in central Africa, in the Egyptian Sinai, in Iraq and Syria, and beyond.

Where are all the weapons in the region, especially in Iraq and Syria, coming from?

The broadly defined Middle East remains one of the most heavily armed regions in the world. Many countries are awash with weapons left over from the Cold War, when the region was a key venue for US-Soviet proxy battles for power and influence. Those included the decade-long Afghanistan war, in which US-backed *mujahideen* challenged the Soviet-backed government. There were also a series of wars internal to the region. The Iran-Iraq war, which raged from 1980 to 1988, resulted in over a million casualties and in enormous social and economic costs as well as long-term political consequences.

The end of the Cold War did not lead to a diminution of arms flooding into the region. Most governments in the region – including absolute monarchies, military or military-backed dictatorships, and partial democracies – continued to rely on powerful militaries and continued to buy and amass large amounts of weapons from abroad. Israel has by far the most powerful military in the region, as well as the only nuclear-weapons arsenal in the Middle East. In addition, since the end of the Cold War the region has seen a series of internal armed battles in several countries, as well as several large-scale international invasions and wars mostly initiated and led by the US. Beginning with Operation Desert Storm in 1991, the first US war against Iraq, and moving through the US invasion of Afghanistan in 2001, then the invasion and long-term occupation of Iraq starting in 2003, the Israeli war against Hizbullah in Lebanon in 2006 followed by the 2011 US/NATO attack and regime change in Libya, the region has seen a virtually unending flood of conventional and high-tech weapons. The US occupation of Iraq and the air war in Libya have been responsible for the majority of the weapons spreading across the Middle East, North Africa, parts of Central Africa and beyond.

In Libya, when the Qadafi government was overthrown, weapons storage facilities and military bases across the country were essentially thrown open, abandoned by their guards, many of whom joined the anti-Qadafi mobilization. The US remained concerned about maintaining control of the chaotic country, awash with weapons, after the killing of Qadafi. In October 2011, then-Secretary of State Hillary Clinton made a telling Freudian slip, describing US 'concern as to how we disarm' the country. Only afterward did she catch herself and correct her statement to 'or how the Libyans disarm everybody who has weapons'.

The problem was that virtually everyone in Libya *did* have weapons – and, rather than being disarmed, many people joined or created militias that turned post-Qadafi Libya into a violent, turbulent country. Two governments competed for power and legitimacy, and a host of militias continued fighting. Some of the most powerful militias were politically identified with al-Qaeda. But the weapons poured out of government warehouses into the hands of militias and out of the country – quickly showing up to fuel conflicts in Iraq and Syria, in Mali, in next-door Egypt and beyond. By early 2015 the situation inside Libya remained chaotic, and the flood of Libyan weapons continued to destabilize the region.

The Iraq war, which continued after the 2011 withdrawal of US troops, saw the rise of a plethora of militias as well as the huge (though largely ineffectual) US-trained Iraqi military and police forces, all armed with billions of dollars' worth of US-provided weapons. With the reprised sectarian civil war that re-emerged around 2009-10 and escalated after the US troop withdrawal the following year, militias of all sorts all found US arms easy to obtain. When the Iraqi military essentially collapsed in response to attacks by ISIS in 2014, huge caches of its weapons were abandoned, lost, sold on the black market, or provided to ISIS by defecting soldiers. Many of those weapons ended up strengthening ISIS as well as the al-Qaeda-linked Nusra Front and some of the smaller opposition forces in both Syria and Iraq.

In Syria, the early militarization of the opposition that began in 2011 was made possible by defecting Syrian soldiers who joined the rebels with their weapons. By 2012 the opposition forces appeared to be growing stronger, with defecting soldiers' own weapons bolstered by access to some heavy arms captured from government bases. Later that year Syrian rebels were reporting a relaxation of the previously strict US rules on what kinds of weapons were allowed across the border, and that portable anti-aircraft missiles had been released from Turkish warehouses where they had been impounded.

In March 2013, Matt Schroeder, who tracks the spread of such weapons for the Federation of American Scientists, said the appearance of modern, sophisticated anti-aircraft missiles in the hands of such fragmented rebel groups was deeply troubling because of their capacity to bring down civilian airlines. 'This is a step above anything we've seen before in the hands of non-state actors,' he said. 'This is a new and unfortunate chapter in recent manpad [man-portable air-defence] proliferation.'

Until September 2014 the US remained officially reluctant to provide arms directly to the anti-Assad rebels. At that time, in the context of the decision to conduct US airstrikes in Syria and Iraq and send troops back to Iraq, the US approved some relatively small-scale arms provisions. But even before that the opposition's weapons were mostly of US manufacture, provided to the rebels by Saudi Arabia and Qatar, Jordan and the UAE, sent into Syria through Turkey. Most of those weapons had been sold to Washington's Gulf allies over the years in multi-billion-dollar arms deals. (France and Britain have sold some weapons to Gulf states as well.)

Despite its official refusal to provide arms, there is no question that the US either approved or discreetly ignored the reality that some of its closest allies in the region were directly providing arms (and money to buy more arms) to the entire range of Syrian opposition forces – 'moderate' and extremist, Islamist and secular, ISIS and Nusra, and beyond. And there is no question that the US chose not to move to stop those sales.

All US weapons sold internationally, including those sold to close allies, contain end-use restrictions. They limit how, where and against whom they can be used, and they restrict whether and to whom the weapons can be resold. There is little doubt that the US could, if it chose, bring an immediate halt to the Saudi, Qatari and other arms shipments heading to the Syrian opposition forces by enforcing those end-use restrictions on pain of losing all future access to US arms.

The Syrian government, of course, has a well-armed and well-trained military, but it has taken serious casualties through the years of the civil war, and many of its weapons have been lost or degraded. Beginning in 2013, it began relying more significantly on military support from Hizbullah fighters from Lebanon – many of whose arms originally came through Syria in the first place. Iran and Russia remain the key military backers of the Syrian military.

While there have been discussions and some UN-based efforts toward a ceasefire (or local ceasefires) in Syria, as of early 2015 those plans had never included the possibility of an arms embargo. Given the centrality of the Syrian civil war to the broader regional and global 'war on terror', there is a clear need for an end to the flood of weapons that continues to escalate the conflict.

Neither side is prepared to offer a unilateral ceasefire. In the context of new negotiations toward a full or partial ceasefire, one possibility would be for the US to call for and support a comprehensive international arms embargo. Washington could announce immediate plans to stop sending or enabling the provision of any arms to any rebel forces and to prevent US allies from doing so, while simultaneously renewing pressure on Russia and Iran to stop sending any arms to the Syrian government side. Washington would have to be prepared to strengthen and enforce end-use agreements on arms exports to exert necessary pressure on its regional allies, including Saudi Arabia, Qatar, the UAE, Turkey, Jordan and Israel. Despite inevitable opposition from US arms manufacturers, the US government would need to make clear to these recipients that if they continue using or providing arms to any side in Syria, the US will cancel all existing weapons contracts with them. The US should make clear in the UN Security Council that it is prepared to support a resolution imposing a complete and enforceable arms embargo on all sides of the Syrian conflict.

Although an arms embargo will not alone solve the problems of ISIS and its cruel power, or the Syrian regime and its repression, or the unaccountable militias destroying the lives of too many ordinary Syrian civilians, no ceasefire can hold while weapons continue to flow. The constant refrain that 'there is no military solution' in Syria or in Iraq remains true – the brutality of ISIS does not change that reality. The use of US weapons – airstrikes, bombings, and more – too often leads to more support for ISIS, not less. (See 'Why did Sunnis support ISIS?') More weapons will continue to make things worse, not better.

6 In the region and the world

Why do so many Middle Eastern governments and opposition movements use religion to justify violence?

In much of the world, for much of history, religion played a powerful, often defining role in political contests, power struggles, conflicts over resources, and wars. In many parts of the world that is still the case: the Buddhist government's oppression of Muslim Rohingyas in Burma, the rebellion of Hindu Tamils against the Buddhist-dominated government of Sri Lanka, attacks on Christians, animists, and others by the Muslim-dominated government in Sudan (which also reflected the divide between Arabs of the north and Black Africans further south). And of course Israeli occupation and apartheid policies are based on privileging Jewish rights over those of non-Jews, whether Muslim or Christian.

Today's wars and conflicts – including internal struggles over power and resources, as well as broad movements against colonialism and imperialism – often are defined in religious and/or sectarian terms. Sunni against Shi'a, 'true' Muslims against apostates, Jews against Muslims, etc. Most of the military struggles and some, though certainly not all, of the social movements mobilized against repressive and anti-democratic governments, against foreign occupation in the region, against Western encroachment, today define themselves in religious/sectarian terms. But as is always the case, the context goes far beyond the claim of 'Muslim' or 'Sunni' or whatever identity.

Like every social movement, every Islamist movement in the Arab world today has its own particular history and political trajectory. Some have much older roots. Egypt's Muslim Brotherhood, arguably the first modern Islamist organization in the region, goes back to the 1930s. But in most of those years the organization and its offshoots across the region were brutally suppressed, with many leaders jailed or driven into exile. In post-Nasser Egypt, there were periods when 'independents' known to be affiliated with the Brotherhood were allowed to run for parliamentary seats, but their influence was never allowed to challenge the secular US-oriented military dictatorships.

Overall, contemporary Islamist movements have all emerged in the context of the failure of earlier efforts to shape the challenges presented by Western colonial and post-colonial intervention and interference, corrupt despotic regimes, chronic impoverishment and unemployment, repression and the denial of human rights. Those failures included the Arab monarchies, Arab nationalism, pan-Arabism, Arab socialism, and pro-Western, globalized Arab neoliberalism. None succeeded at ending poverty, protecting human rights, or ensuring 'bread, freedom, and dignity', as many of the protesters in Egypt's Tahrir Square demanded. None guaranteed the rights of citizenship for ordinary people.

It was largely in response to those failures that the narrative of political religion – Islamism – took hold as the mobilizing force bringing people into the streets. Beginning with the Iranian revolution of 1979 that over-threw the US-backed Shah and brought a Shi'a Islamic force to power under the Ayatollah Khomeini, political Islam has played a major role in shaping political momentum across the Middle East. After the first Gulf War against Iraq in 1991, and in the midst of a major economic crisis spurred by the diminishing price of oil, the Islamic Salvation Front, or FIS, was elected in Algeria, supplanting for the first time since independence the secular model of the anti-colonial National Liberation Front.

In some countries, colonial powers imposed religious or sectarian governing structures on local populations. In Lebanon, for example, in 1926 during the Mandate period, France imposed what was known as a confessional system, in which numbers of seats in the parliament, as well as specific positions (president, prime minister, etc) were assigned to each of the 6 separate Muslim and 12 separate Christian sects. When Lebanon won its independence in 1943, France withdrew, but the confessional system remained and it remains today, still based on the last census, which was taken in 1936.

There is no question that the relative size of Lebanon's populations of various sects has changed. Christians are no longer anywhere close to the number of Muslims; Shi'a significantly outnumber Sunni, but fear of demographic instability, especially after the 1975-90 civil war, has resulted in a refusal to conduct a new census. Many Lebanese still identify with sect-based political and even military forces that continue to supersede national identity, although significant political shifts have occurred. The Shi'a-based Hizbullah movement rose in 1982, splitting from the traditional Shi'a Amal party to launch a more militant challenge to the Israeli occupation of Lebanon. Some Christians now support Hizbullah, and there are reports of other parties organizing outside their traditional sectarian base. The consequence of colonial occupation remains, and what exists today is less a direct religious conflict than a power struggle in which religion is used to mobilize support for power grabs and violence against other groups.

If one looks at Iraq, the defeat of the monarchy in the late 1950s set the stage for the nationalist and pan-Arab regime of Saddam Hussein. An Iraqi Shi'a majority, with large Sunni Arab and Kurdish minorities and smaller communities of Christians, Yazidis, Turkomans and others lived in relatively cosmopolitan circumstances, although Sunnis held disproportionately privileged positions in the military and government. Until 1991 Iraq was a modern secular society, with a large urban middle class. Iraqis, at least in the cities, had access to most economic and social rights, including advanced education and healthcare and relative equality for women, but also confronted a government known for its denial of most political and civil rights. Political opponents, communists, supporters of Kurdish nationalism, Shi'a marsh dwellers and others faced vicious repression, including arbitrary arrests, torture and extra-judicial killing.

Like its Baath Party counterpart in Syria, the Iraqi Baathists were ruthlessly secular. In both countries, minority communities – Sunnis in Iraq, Alawites (a branch of Shi'a Islam) in Syria – were disproportionately privileged in state patronage systems. Neither the Alawite al-Assad family in Syria nor the Sunni Saddam Hussein in Iraq had any interest in building Alawite or Sunni religious governance in their countries; both were secular as could be. But both used religious identity to divide and control populations, and to apportion political and economic rights and privileges.

After its first war against Iraq in 1991, the US imposed 12 years of crippling economic sanctions on the country. The impact was genocidal, including the death of over half a million children, the destruction of much of the physical and intellectual infrastructure of the country, the shredding of the social fabric, and the collapse of much of Iraqis' national identity. Many Iraqis responded by turning even further away from the national toward smaller, more local identities shaped by religion, sect, ethnicity and tribe.

Immediately following its second invasion and occupation in 2003, the US ordered the dissolution of Iraq's military and its civil service, thus destroying the most secular and nationalist institutions in the country, and leaving several million Iraqis bereft of their longstanding national identity as well as their jobs. The US occupation authorities imposed a new political system in which power was apportioned to sectarian political parties ostensibly based on the size of various religious and ethnic communities in Iraq.

As the US war and occupation dragged on, ethnicity, tribe, and especially religion became newly important in the assertion of Iraqis' identity and in their search for protection. So sectarian identity became the basis not only for the newly empowered US-backed Shi'a-dominated government, but for conflicts over land and money, control of oil and other resources and political power. By the mid-2000s, those conflicts looked increasingly like a sectarian civil war.

In the Gaza Strip, the history of the Islamist Hamas movement reflects a different trajectory still. Hamas emerged in 1988, in the first months of the first Palestinian intifada or uprising. Its political and ideological origins go back much further, reflecting the influence of the Egyptian Muslim Brotherhood, but it was only in the context of the uprising that Hamas emerged as an organizational reality. Israel encouraged Hamas's rise to power, counting on the religious movement to somehow reduce the power of the intifada and the influence of the secular nationalist Palestine Liberation Organization that Israel then defined as its top enemy. Former Israeli official Avner Cohen, who was responsible for religious affairs in Gaza until 1994, told the *Wall Street Journal*: 'Hamas, to my great regret, is Israel's creation.' The popular appeal of Hamas quickly grew. Like so many other Islamist organizations, it first gained support less for its ideology than by providing the impoverished population with desperately needed services unavailable under the Israeli occupation: clinics, schools, summer camps, social and economic assistance, and more. It was only later, by the mid- to late-1990s, as poverty and immiseration hit Gaza especially hard, that many more in the population turned more toward religion, and the Islamist approach to social life advocated by Hamas won new adherents.

Similar trajectories emerged in many other countries, some of them much earlier. On a broader regional level, other factors were at work too. In countries where governments define themselves and claim legitimacy in religious terms (Saudi Arabia being the clearest example), as well as some of the military dictatorships in the region (such as Egypt under Hosni Mubarak), human rights, such as the rights of free speech and association, are often denied. In those situations, the mosque was often the only place to meet and opposition forces often adopted religious approaches. The same demand for 'bread, freedom and dignity' that mobilized so many in Egypt rang out, with an overlay – often a very thin overlay – of religion.

There are specific push-and-pull factors as well. In the context of the Syrian civil war, for instance, many secular anti-Assad fighters, faced with an intractable enemy in Damascus and simultaneously challenged by much more powerful Islamist forces, such as ISIS, chose to abandon the US-backed Free Syrian Army or other ostensibly 'moderate' militias to join ISIS. This weakened the secular forces, of course, and the additional fighters accelerated the strength and popularity of ISIS. By 2013 or so, ISIS was wealthier (from illicit oil sales, kidnap ransoms, 'taxes' imposed on people and businesses in territory it controlled, and other sources) and better armed than any of the secular anti-Assad forces. So it was not surprising that some of the formerly secular fighters switched loyalties and joined ISIS – not because of a sudden conversion to the ISIS extreme brand of Islam, but despite it, because ISIS offered higher salaries, better weapons, and occasional military victories. In many cases fighters would follow local leaders, powerbrokers who shifted loyalties between various militias, and brought their followers with them.

Of course, in many of these scenarios jihadist organizations use the veneer of religious orthodoxy simply to claim legitimacy for violent, brutal actions. Like Judaism, Christianity and pretty much every other religion, Islam's sacred texts include language that can be interpreted to allow or even encourage violence. The Torah calls for death by stoning for blasphemy; the New Testament legitimizes slavery. While many Islamic scholars have made clear that some claims of Quranic authority made by ISIS – for actions like condoning death as punishment for depicting a likeness of the

Prophet – are completely false, there is no doubt that language approving extreme punishment exists in all the holy texts, reflecting the mores of ancient societies. But there is also no question that religion is being severely misused in today's Syria, Iraq, Saudi Arabia and beyond.

What is the Sunni-Shi'a split in the region all about?

While the legacies of colonialism, wars, and struggles over resources continue to shape the broad conflicts in the Middle East, a significant part of the conflict is rooted in the sectarian schism between Sunni and Shi'a Muslims. One of the eight separate conflicts that make up the Syrian civil war is the regional struggle between Sunni and Shi'a powers, a struggle played out with Saudi Arabia and Iran as the primary combatants. Patrick Cockburn subtitled his 2014 book 'ISIS and the New Sunni Uprising'. Much of the mid-2000s civil war, as well as the revived post-2013 fighting in Iraq, reflects the sectarian divide set in place by the US in 2003 when it invaded and overthrew the Sunni-dominated Iraqi government, dismantled the military and civil service in which Sunnis had long been privileged, and supported a new government in which the once relatively marginalized but majority Shi'a took over and governed on a thoroughly sectarian basis.

There is of course a theological basis to the split, the original divide within Islam. It began with a struggle over succession – who should be the leader of the Muslim community after the death of the Prophet Muhammad. The two sides each supported a different candidate – Abu Bakr, who had been a close colleague of Muhammad and was thought by many to be the best qualified to lead the community (although he was also Muhammad's father-in-law, that was not considered important), versus Ali ibn Abi Talib, who was related to Muhammad by blood (he was a cousin) and by marriage (he was also his son-in-law) and was supported by those who believed that there was a divine order to the succession.

The Sunnis are identified as followers of the *sunna*, or the way, referring to the Qur'an's description of how leaders should be selected. The word Shi'a comes from *si'atu Ali*, or 'partisans of Ali'. Ali became caliph for five years, then was assassinated, and the caliphate which had been based in what is now Saudi Arabia shifted to the dynasties ruling in Damascus and Baghdad. The Shi'as, who had followed Ali, opposed those rulers, and, in a later battle in the Iraqi city of Karbala, Ali's son Husayn and many of his followers were killed by the soldiers of those caliphates. Karbala became a kind of symbolic centre of Shi'a Islam, and following the battle – really a massacre of Shi'as – the split became stronger. Sunnis became the large majority, and Shi'as continued to be marginalized and oppressed. Today, Sunnis remain the vast majority of the world's Muslims (most estimates indicate 80-85 per cent to be Sunni and 15-20 per cent Shi'a).

Is this conflict just an intractable war between two Islamic sects intent on imposing their beliefs on the populace?

Though it may seem unlikely, it's not primarily religion that has made these groups mortal enemies. The contemporary Shi'a-Sunni divide is about power. Theocratic governments in Iran and Saudi Arabia impose versions of Shi'a or Sunni orthodoxy, respectively, on their populations, but other Muslim governments identify with one or the other sect largely in the context of political power and identity privilege. That is, the Sunni governments of Jordan, Qatar, Bahrain, the UAE, Turkey, Oman and other countries privilege Sunni communities, often discriminate against their Shi'a populations (even when, as in Sunni-governed Bahrain, the Shi'a are actually the majority of the population) – but not with the goal of imposing rigid Sunni orthodoxy on the country. In

Shi'a-dominated Iraq and in Syria, where the ruling family is Alawite, a branch of Shi'ism, Sunnis are often discriminated against, sometimes brutally, but, again, the governments have no interest in imposing Shi'a interpretations of Islamic law or traditions on largely secular populations. In Shi'a-majority Bahrain, the Sunni monarchy brutally suppressed the democratic protesters of the 2011 Arab Spring uprising, and it continues to jail human rights activists and other government critics, almost all of whom are Shi'a – but the goal is preservation of the US-backed monarchy's absolute power over the population, not the imposition of Sunni practices.

In the foregoing cases, the contemporary Sunni-Shi'a split has much more to do with identity politics within the countries and the struggles for power and hegemony in the region. Over the last 50 years or so in the Middle East, only two countries possessed all three of the requirements to be indigenous (as opposed to derivative, such as Israel) regional powers: oil for wealth, size of land and population, and sufficient water. Those were Iraq and Iran. With the essential destruction of Iraq's economic and military power following 12 years of sanctions and a decade of war and occupation, Iran emerged as an uncontested regional power. It was in this context that George W Bush's administration transformed the long-hostile US position toward Iran dating from the overthrow of the US-backed Shah into full-scale 'axis of evil' efforts at undermining the Iranian economy and covertly supporting regime change in Tehran.

Where does Saudi Arabia fit in?

Saudi Arabia, the largest, wealthiest and most powerful of the Gulf petro-monarchies, used its oil wealth to influence regional developments, maintain its strategic ties to the US, and build unacknowledged but strong ties with Israel – all largely under the public radar. It also spent billions on building and staffing *madrassas*, or

Islamic schools, across the region and around the world, part of a large-scale campaign to win political as well as religious support for its brand of extreme Wahhabi Islam (see 'What is Wahhabism?'). Riyadh long saw Iran as its strategic challenger for dominance in the Middle East (which explains much of its cosiness with Israel). But again, until about 2011 it was all under the table.

Saudi Arabia did not come forward publicly to lead a regional Sunni coalition against the Iran-led Shi'a grouping of Syria, Iraq and Hizbullah in Lebanon until the Syrian uprising against the Assad regime was morphing into a multifaceted civil war. And in the context of that civil war, the overt regional power struggle between Riyadh and Tehran – for control of oil markets and pipelines and beyond – paralleled a sectarian battle between those same forces for positioning as the most important global voice of Islam.

The current version of Washington's global war on terror, and the battle against ISIS, takes place in the context of the wider regional sectarian battle already under way. In Iraq, where it is perhaps most concentrated, the large Sunni minority, disenfranchised from their privileged position when the US invaded and demolished the Iraqi civil service and military, has faced more than a decade of Shi'a-dominated and increasingly sectarian US-backed governments in Baghdad. Nuri al-Maliki, of Iraq's Shi'a Dawa Party, became prime minister in 2006, just as the sectarian civil war was exploding across the country alongside the anti-occupation resistance. Instead of moving to reduce the tensions, Maliki immediately enforced his own sectarian policies. His ministries of defence and intelligence, especially, were infamous for widespread brutality against individual Sunnis and Sunni communities, including mass arrests, torture in prisons, extra-judicial executions, even bombing of Sunni areas.

Not surprisingly, anti-government mobilization among Sunnis grew, rooted in the existing resentments of a community that had been consciously sidelined and faced continued discrimination during the years of US occupation and US-backed governments. That was the context in 2013, when ISIS suddenly rose to power. There was a shockingly high level of tolerance, even support for the extremist organization, even among largely secular Sunni communities, who saw ISIS as the lesser evil, a potential ally with better arms to defend Sunni communities against the continuing ravages of their own Shi'a-sectarian government.

It was for that reason that so many ISIS military strategists, trainers and commanders are reported to come from the embittered Sunni former generals of Iraq's Saddam Hussein-era Baathist military. And, for the same reason, every US airstrike or drone attack against ISIS fighters holed up in a Sunni community somewhere (a strike that might be greeted in the US with a cheer of 'Yay, we got the bad guys') is greeted with an angry 'There go the Americans again, bombing Sunnis in the interest of the Shi'a and the Kurds'. So even though the Obama administration might claim that the US military war against ISIS must be matched by a political campaign to win Sunnis away from ISIS, the military strikes are actually ensuring the failure of any such political effort.

An early March 2015 military campaign to oust ISIS from the overwhelmingly Sunni city of Tikrit, which it had occupied since June 2014, provides an example of the longer-term effect of the sectarian actions of war. Tikrit, the second-largest Iraqi city controlled by ISIS, is on the road from Baghdad to Mosul, the largest ISIS-occupied city. Along with its strategic significance, Tikrit was also important as a symbol: as the birthplace of Saddam Hussein, it held special significance for many Sunnis. The attack was launched against Tikrit primarily by pro-government Iraqi Shi'a militias mostly trained by Iran, backed by airstrikes from the Iraqi military.

A reporter from McClatchy News Service told the BBC on 2 March 2015 that much of the population of the city had already fled. Describing the effect of the bombing and artillery strikes, he sounded a warning very familiar from the days of the war in Vietnam – 'I don't know if they're going to liberate the city so much as destroy it,' he said. If and when Tikrit's Sunni residents return to their ravaged city, it remains very uncertain whether they will hold ISIS, or their own government and its allied sectarian militias, responsible for the destruction.

By late 2015 the military involvement of Washington's Arab 'partners' in the US-led coalition against ISIS was dwindling. A front-page 8 November headline in the *New York Times* acknowledged that 'As US Escalates Air War On ISIS, Allies Slip Away.' It reported that while the Gulf Arab allies continued to arm a wide array of rebel forces in Syria, including some of the most extreme Islamist organizations, their direct participation in the air and ground war was rapidly diminishing. Like earlier US-crafted 'coalitions' designed to provide an Arab or international credential for a US military campaign, this one was rapidly devolving back to a war of the US and its closest Western allies.

What are the consequences of the Syrian war across the region?

Understanding the consequences of Syria's multi-sided civil war is much easier than understanding the dynamics that shaped and perpetuate it. The war has not resulted in any one side – neither the Syrian regime, nor the diverse array of anti-Assad opposition factions, nor ISIS – winning clear influence. Rather, military initiative and political positions have shifted back and forth among the contending forces and their regional and global backers.

The regime's defeats at the hands of various opposition forces have meant it no longer has the power to govern large swaths of Syrian territory. That has set in place a division of the country into a variety of constantly shifting fiefdoms and micro-states that threatens the very existence of Syria as a unified nation-state. The Syrian divisions – some of which are grounded in sectarian and/or ethnic rifts – parallel the collapse of the long-unified Iraqi state into a mosaic of ethnically and religiously divided cantons created at gunpoint during Iraq's sectarian civil war of the mid-2000s.

The years of the Syrian war have also seen the rise of violent extremists, both Islamist and secular, whose organizations have taken advantage of the power vacuum in local and regional areas. That has resulted from the overwhelming discrediting and/or defeat of the regime in many areas and thus the loss of its ability to rule, plus the internal fighting inside the anti-Assad opposition, whose disunity renders it largely incapable of governing as well. The emergence of these new extremists – including ISIS – has also risen and fallen along with the growing or diminishing power of the regime and the opposition.

What has remained constant is the downward spiral of humanitarian disaster that has characterized Syria since very early in the conflict: deaths and injuries of hundreds of thousands, the creation of millions of refugees and internally displaced, the massive destruction of whole cities, including millennia-old historic and cultural sites, and the shredding of Syria's once-advanced and relatively egalitarian social fabric.

As of October 2015, the United Nations estimated that over 250,000 had died in the war. Many of these were of course civilians – horrifyingly killed in 'barrel bomb' attacks (crude weapons made of barrels stuffed with explosives, dropped from helicopters or planes with deadly impact, mainly on civilians) by Syrian government forces, in the shelling of cities by both government and opposition sides, in US and allied airstrikes ostensibly aimed at ISIS fighters. By mid-October 2015 the Syrian Observatory for Human Rights, London-based and largely pro-opposition, reported that at least 12,517 children had been killed, along with 8,062 women.

But many of those killed in the war have also been

combatants on all sides – a reality largely ignored by US government officials and the mainstream US media, which consistently references total casualty figures as something for which the Assad regime is solely responsible. In the middle of 2013, for example, the Syrian Observatory calculated that 60 per cent of the war dead were fighters. According to its calculations, 43 per cent of the deaths were of Syrian military and police forces along with pro-government militias. The next-largest contingent was that of civilian non-combatants, who made up 37 per cent. Making up the smallest sector were opposition fighters, including civilians who had taken up arms as well as military defectors and foreign fighters, at 17 per cent.

Most aid organizations inside Syria were increasingly unable to provide basic services because of the expansion of the war and the failure of all sides to abide by international legal requirements for humanitarian access to civilians on all sides. ISIS in particular, and other extremist organizations to a lesser degree, continued to target humanitarian workers without regard to international law. Numerous aid workers were kidnapped, some were killed.

The dead and wounded were almost entirely inside Syria. But the humanitarian disaster rooted in the Syrian civil war spread far beyond Syria's borders. The UN's Office for Coordination of Humanitarian Affairs (OCHA) appeal for humanitarian relief in 2015 was for $26.7 million – but by early November only a little more than $10 million had been raised. The numbers are staggering. More than half of Syria's 23 million people have been forced to flee their homes because of the war. More than four million Syrians have become refugees in Jordan, Turkey, Lebanon, Egypt, Iraq and outside the region. Another seven million are displaced within Syria.

In December 2014 the UN High Commissioner for Refugees said, 'Syria's war is still escalating and the humanitarian situation is becoming protracted. Refugees and internally displaced people have exhausted their savings and resources, and host countries are at breaking point. We need a new aid architecture that links support to the refugees with what is being done to stabilize the communities who host them.'

But the chance of reaching that goal of 'a new aid architecture' remained remote. The 2014 $8.4-billion assistance request from the UN refugee agency included, for the first time, aid to 'over a million vulnerable people in host countries', meaning that it aimed to provide direct support to at least the poorer of the countries hosting large numbers of Syrian refugees: Egypt, Lebanon and Jordan. But as had been the case so many times in the past, the UN humanitarian agencies remained unable to obtain the money needed. The crisis in those neighbouring countries has been dramatic. By 2015, the 1.1 million Syrian refugees in Lebanon made up one-fifth of the population, with consequences that went beyond job scarcity to potentially threaten the very fragile demographic balance between diverse and competing ethnic and religious groups. In the desert kingdom of Jordan, a longstanding crisis of water scarcity was seriously exacerbated by an influx of more than 630,000 Syrian refugees. Turkey, a relatively wealthy though increasingly conflict-torn country, had managed to absorb almost 2 million Syrian refugees by September 2015, but its capacity by the end of the year was nearing its limit.

What is the European refugee crisis all about?

As the war in Syria escalated and conditions for Syrian civilians deteriorated drastically in 2014 and 2015, far more Syrians were forced to flee their homes and much higher numbers moved to find refuge outside the region, braving gruelling border crossings and dangerous sea journeys to get to Europe, the majority by rickety boat from Turkey to various Greek islands, much smaller numbers attempting to reach Italy from

Libya. By early November 2015, over 750,000 desperate Syrian refugees had sought safety in Europe, most of them arriving in Greece and attempting various, often closed-off routes to central and ultimately northern Europe, with most hoping to reach Germany or Sweden, perceived as the most welcoming of the often inhospitable EU countries.

The dramatic escalation in numbers of refugees attempting this journey – some dying along the way – began earlier in 2015. Some European countries, particularly the newer members of the EU in eastern and central Europe, refused to accept refugees, rapidly constructing border fences and barriers to keep out thousands of desperate Syrians arriving daily, often on foot, walking from Turkey through the Balkans, into Hungary, perhaps the least welcoming, to Austria and on towards Germany and Sweden. For some months the countries most immediately affected, Italy and especially Greece, facing its own economic and political crises, were largely ignored by allies and neighbouring states.

In early September the image of a small boy, a Syrian Kurd whose body washed up on the Turkish shore when the smugglers' boat his family was in sank off the coast, captured the hearts of people across Europe and the US, resulting in an outpouring of new attention and efforts to build support for the huge number of refugees. Suddenly the European refugee crisis eclipsed the continuing and far larger crisis facing Syrians seeking refuge in the region – especially in Turkey, Lebanon and Jordan.

In an important effort to reduce the hysteria gripping many European politicians and others, the EU's foreign policy chief, Federica Mogherini, noted on 2 October: 'This is not just a European crisis; it is a regional and global crisis. If you look at the number of Syrians, you have eight million internally displaced people still in Syria and four million in Turkey, Lebanon and Jordan. You have something like 350,000 refugees in Europe... One number tells everything: the percentage of refugees of the total population of Europe is 0.1 per cent. In Lebanon, it is 25 per cent of the population. We have to put things in perspective. The issue is manageable for us Europeans.'

Germany offered to accept up to 800,000 refugees in 2015, although by November efforts were under way to cut back on how many were actually allowed in. Attempts to craft an EU-wide collective response stalled, as central and eastern European countries, led by rightist forces in Hungary, rejected the obligation to accept specified numbers of refugees.

The US remained the outlier, accepting only about 1,000 refugees in 2015. The Obama administration, under growing public pressure, agreed in late October to allow 10,000 Syrian refugees, but made clear it would not change the existing onerous vetting process, under which every Syrian (and others) requesting asylum faced up to two years of interviews, production of documents, waiting and more. It was grounded in a post-9/11 policy that assumes every Syrian, Afghan, Iraqi, or Palestinian refugee, including children, pregnant women and old people, must be a terrorist – until she or he can prove otherwise. Refugee assistance and anti-war organizations mobilized to demand that the Obama administration accept at least 100,000 asylum-seekers, but as 2015 drew to a close, the White House showed no indication it would consider anything close to that number.

What is Iran's role in the US global war on terror?

The 2003 overthrow of Saddam Hussein's government in Iraq by the US was a great boon to Iran in its strategic competition for regional hegemony. For decades, Iran and Iraq were the only two countries in the Middle East with all three of the key requirements for indigenous power: oil for wealth, size of land and population, and water. The two had competed for years, and for almost a decade in the 1980s fought a bitter war. The US provided arms to both sides, but tilted towards Iraq (providing seed stock for bio-weapons and satellite targeting intelligence for chemical weapons, among other things) because it was the weaker of the two, and it served US interests to have the two potential regional challengers fighting each other.

The Iran-Iraq war left over a million people dead in the two countries. With the years of US wars, sanctions and occupation, Iraq was largely destroyed, leaving Iran without its traditional challenger. That brought it even more directly into the longstanding US crosshairs. Iran had been targeted since the overthrow of the US-installed and US-backed Shah and the creation of the Islamic Republic in 1979.

(In the early 2000s, Turkey emerged as a potential regional power, having managed to create the 17th-largest economy in the world without oil. With its size and copious water, that newly created wealth brought Turkey into the regional power mix as well. But as a NATO member and longtime US ally, Turkey's rising power – even under the leadership of the Islamist-oriented Justice and Development Party of prime minister and then President Recep Tayyip Erdogan – did not shift the US strategic focus on challenging Iran.)

When the US overthrew the Iraqi government and political system in 2003, the replacement was not a popular egalitarian democracy, but rather a thoroughly sectarian system of political parties based on the various ethnic and religious communities in Iraq's multi-faceted population. The Shi'a majority, who had long faced discrimination at the hands of the Sunni-led (though ruthlessly secular) government of Saddam Hussein, took power with US support, as Washington's occupation authority forcibly disbanded the Iraqi military and civil service. The sectarian struggle that resulted escalated to full-scale civil war by the mid-2000s, waged alongside the continuing war against US occupation. From quite early in the US occupation, Iran emerged as a major supporter of the US-backed Shi'a-led government, leading many analysts to conclude that the US war in Iraq had benefited Iran more than any other country in the region.

Iran has had a nuclear-power programme since the 1950s, largely because the US convinced the Shah's government, which was reluctant to invest in nuclear energy when it had what appeared to be an endless supply of oil, that it needed to diversify its energy sources. Iran ratified the Nuclear Non-Proliferation Treaty (NPT) in 1970, resulting in longstanding ongoing inspections of its enrichment and other nuclear activities by the UN's nuclear watchdog agency, the IAEA. Under the terms of Article IV of the NPT, Iran, like all non-nuclear weapons states, has 'the inalienable right of all the Parties to the Treaty to develop research, production and use of nuclear energy for peaceful purposes without discrimination'.

As far back as 2007 all 16 US intelligence agencies issued a joint National Intelligence Estimate (NIE) stating that Iran did not have nuclear weapons and, crucially, had not made the political/strategic decision to build a nuclear weapon. The NIE also affirmed earlier reports that Iran had abandoned any past research aimed at militarization or weaponization of its nuclear material back in 2003. In 2012 the NIE's conclusions were reaffirmed by the intelligence community.

But at the political level, despite the intelligence consensus that Tehran was not trying to build a nuclear weapon, Iran remained a consistent and public enemy of the US. Despite close Iranian collaboration with the US during the initial invasion and overthrow of the Taliban in Afghanistan in 2001 after the 9/11 attacks, especially in establishing the US-backed transitional government in Afghanistan in December 2001, the Bush administration identified Iran as a strategic enemy in the global war on terror. In his state of the union address of January 2002, Bush linked Iran with Iraq and North Korea in a so-called 'axis of evil', ending the co-operation that had characterized US-Iran relations for months earlier.

Anti-Iran rhetoric as well as serious cyber-attacks against Iran jointly involving the US and Israel continued through the years of the global war on terror under both the Bush and Obama administrations. Once the Iraqi government was overthrown, and throughout the years of the Iraq war in all its iterations, Israel kept up efforts to target Iran as a major enemy. Claims that Iran's nuclear programme ostensibly represented an 'existential threat' to Israel became a key component of Israeli leaders' efforts to keep US-led international sanctions on Iran. Those efforts, and the constant drumbeat of 'Iran is a threat to Israel' helped deter any pressure that might have been brought to bear on Israel regarding its violations of human rights and international law in its occupation and apartheid policies towards the Palestinians.

When ISIS, in its earlier iteration as al-Qaeda in Iraq (AQI) and then Islamic State in Iraq (ISI) first emerged in 2004, it was one of many Sunni militias fighting alongside Shi'a militias against the US occupation and US-backed Iraqi forces. Many of the Sunni militias shifted loyalties during the 2006 Sunni Awakening campaign, in which the US began paying them to fight on the side of the US and the Iraqi government rather than against them. But ISI never joined the Awakening movement, and continued its anti-US and anti-Baghdad attacks, alongside many Shi'a militias.

While Shi'a Iran continued to provide political and sometimes more concrete support to the US-backed Shi'a-dominated government in Baghdad, it also funded and supported numerous independent Shi'a militias. When the US troop pull-out from Iraq began in 2010 and 2011, ISI didn't disappear, but its influence was significantly diminished. By the time it re-emerged in its later form, as ISIS, first in Syria and then back in Iraq, the Sunni militias that had been part of the Awakening movement had been abandoned by the US-backed government in Baghdad, and were once again part of an insurgency rising across Iraq.

By this time, around 2011 and 2012, Iran was playing a major role in simultaneously supporting both the US-backed Shi'a government in Baghdad and the Shi'a militias that were now fighting alongside the government against what had become a Sunni rebellion. ISIS became more powerful in the chaos of the Syrian civil war, and especially during its dramatic land-grabs of 2014 in both Iraq and Syria. At that point Iran supported the Shi'a government and Shi'a militias against ISIS in Iraq, as well as supporting (as it had for many years) the Alawite (an off-shoot of Shi'a Islam) government of Bashar al-Assad in Syria against ISIS and the Sunni forces supporting it.

So by 2014 Iran was fighting on the same side as the US – against ISIS in both Iraq and Syria – despite the longstanding US-Iran enmity. At the same time and into 2015, Washington and Tehran were engaged in the final year of a long diplomatic process between Iran and what was known as the P-5 + 1 (the five Permanent Members of the UN Security Council – Britain, China, France, Russia, and the US – plus Germany) to resolve disputes over Iran's nuclear-power programme and end the sanctions imposed on it. But negotiations or not, public antagonism towards Iran and opposition to a potential nuclear accord remained rampant in key political and media circles in the US.

Escalating threats from Israel, based on false claims of Iran's supposed nuclear danger (while refusing to acknowledge Israel's own decades-old arsenal of 100 to 300 uninspected nuclear weapons) and thinly veiled threats from Tel Aviv to launch a unilateral war or pressure the US to join a war against Iran, ratcheted up political pressure in the US as well. A highly partisan and electorally driven speech in the US Congress by then-Israeli Prime Minister Binyamin Netanyahu just weeks before the culmination of the Iran nuclear negotiations, accused the Obama administration of appeasement in the face of a supposed Iranian danger, and renewed threats of war.

But at the same time Iran was playing an ever-more influential role in the military struggle against ISIS. In March 2015, Iraq's military and the even stronger Shi'a militias launched an offensive to retake the Sunni-majority city of Tikrit, known as the birthplace of Saddam Hussein, from ISIS control. The militias were largely armed and trained by Iran, and the offensive against Tikrit was commanded directly by Iranian General Qasem Soleimani, who had once led the elite Quds Force of Iran's Revolutionary Guard.

In official Washington circles, the two conflict-driven processes – the tense multilateral negotiations over Iran's nuclear programme and sanctions on the one hand, and Iran's central role on the US side in the war against ISIS on the other hand – were rarely discussed together. In fact the Iranian role in the anti-ISIS war was rarely mentioned at all.

In early April 2015, negotiators in Lausanne won an important victory, agreeing on a framework deal. Both sides made concessions, though Iran gave up far more, accepting an agreement in which US and European sanctions would remain until the UN's nuclear watchdog agency verified Iranian compliance with its new nuclear obligations, and accepting severe cuts in nuclear infrastructure and unprecedentedly intrusive new inspections.

The plan was to reach a final agreement by 30 June. Negotiations proceeded, with hardline elements in both the US Congress and Iran's parliament continuing to oppose any compromise. The deadline was extended several times, talks continued around the clock, and on 14 July exhausted diplomats announced the Joint Comprehensive Plan of Action had been accepted – a huge victory for diplomacy over war.

Under the terms of the deal, Iran agreed to eliminate its entire stockpile of medium-enriched uranium, reduce its low-enriched uranium by 98 per cent, and remove the reactor core of (and in fact fill with concrete) its single plutonium-producing heavy-water reactor. It agreed that for 15 years it will reduce its centrifuges by two-thirds, keeping only its oldest, first-generation ones in use, and will not build any new enrichment facilities. It accepted regular, intrusive 24/7 access for UN inspectors at all Iranian nuclear facilities, and full access to any other venue deemed suspicious. And Iran remains under the permanent obligations of the Nuclear Non-Proliferation Treaty. In return, once the UN watchdog agency IAEA verifies it is abiding by its obligations, nuclear-related sanctions imposed by the US, the EU and the United Nations will be lifted.

While the deal was accepted unquestionably by most of the P-5 + 1 governments, the Obama administration gave Congress a 60-day window to disapprove the agreement, and hardliners continued their efforts to undermine it. The White House fought back, and the strong pro-diplomacy movement in the US, that had already been working to support the deal, rose again to keep the pressure on Congress not to undermine the agreement. By 10 September the pressure bore fruit, and enough senators, all of them Democrats, blocked a procedural vote that would have led to 'disapproval' of the deal. The deal was approved.

While US intelligence agencies had agreed for years that Iran did not have a nuclear weapons programme and indeed had not even made the political decision as to whether it wanted to build a nuclear weapon, the deal still ended what had become a very real, politically motivated, threat of war with Iran. It was thus an historic victory for diplomacy over war, providing a concrete, indisputable refutation of the war supporters' claims that diplomacy was a strategy of the weak, and that it could never accomplish what war could achieve.

The nuclear deal, signalling a major reduction of US-Iran hostility, could set the stage for an entirely new set of diplomatic relationships and alliances in the Middle East. The deal allowed a major US concession in late October, when Washington agreed to Iran's participation in a new round of multilateral negotiations to end the Syria war. In the future, it could set the stage for a real, if still likely unacknowledged, US-Iranian partnership in Baghdad aimed at forcing an end to sectarianism and a move towards real inclusivity by the Iraqi government, accountable largely to Tehran while being armed and financed by Washington. That could encourage an end to Sunni communal support for ISIS as well as support for other extremist elements, both Sunni and Shi'a, across Iraq.

Further on, such a US-Iran rapprochement could eventually lead to a real normalization of relations between the US, its allies and Iran. And, with the end of the conflict over Iran's nuclear-power programme, the nuclear deal could also enable the creation and enforcement of a Middle East free from nuclear weapons – free, indeed, from all weapons of mass destruction – with no exceptions, including Israel's undeclared nuclear arsenal.

What role does oil play in all this?

Oil is at the root of the ISIS crisis for several reasons. Start with the century-old reality that the strategic value of the entire Middle East region, the reason wealthy and powerful countries care much more about war or instability in Middle Eastern countries than a conflict in Cameroon or Sri Lanka is because of the Middle East's massive oil reserves. Oil keeps global capitalism afloat.

Since 1967, US foreign policy interests in the region have remained tripartite: oil, Israel and strategic power-projection. These elements were all present in the early 1970s, when, as religious history scholar Karen Armstrong wrote, the 'soaring oil price created by the 1973 embargo – when Arab petroleum producers cut off supplies to the US to protest against the Americans' military support for Israel – gave the kingdom all the petrodollars it needed to export its idiosyncratic form of Islam'. And of course Saudi Wahhabism lies at the root of the ISIS brand of radical Islamist extremism. More recently, while it's clear that the US invasion and occupation of Iraq in 2003 had many causes, one of the most important involved oil.

And that US occupation of Iraq set the precise conditions for the emergence of ISIS. As ISIS continues its territorial expansion and the US remains at war against it, oil serves to enrich the Islamist organization. It connects ISIS to its putative enemies in Iraq, Syria and beyond, and provides a potential weapon of diplomatic pressure.

When the renamed ISIS re-emerged in Syria in 2011 and moved to seize cities and territory across northern Syria and western Iraq, oil – producing it, refining it, and selling it – became a core component of its financial survival. Syria was never a major oil producer by Middle Eastern standards, but its relatively small fields still accounted for about a quarter of the Syrian economy. By September 2014, according to *Business Insider*, ISIS was 'cutting deals with local traders and buyers, even businessmen who support Syrian President Bashar al-Assad, and some of its oil has made its way back to government buyers through a series of middlemen. "Islamic State makes not less than $2 million daily that allows them to pay salaries and maintain their operations," said a former Western oil executive who worked in a foreign oil firm operating in Syria before the crisis and who is familiar with the nascent oil market.'

One of the ironies of the multifaceted Syrian civil war is the degree to which trade and economic relations between the various sides continue, even amidst the brutal fighting. In the case of ISIS-controlled oil, the traders seeking profits from Syrian crude, sometimes refined using small-scale equipment smuggled into the country, find themselves buying from the extremist Islamist organization fighting against the Syrian government, then turning around to sell to businesspeople close to the Assad regime. Government officials in Syria also engage directly with ISIS across areas it controls to jointly protect access to electricity, water and sometimes transportation.

In Iraq, where oil reserves are among the highest in the world and the territory under its control includes some of Iraq's productive fields, ISIS quickly became one of the richest insurgent organizations in the world. By November 2014, according to *The Guardian*,

ISIS had consolidated its grip on oil supplies in Iraq and now presides over a sophisticated smuggling empire with illegal exports going to Turkey, Jordan and Iran, according to smugglers and Iraqi officials. Six months after it grabbed vast swaths of territory, the radical militant group is earning millions of dollars a week from its Iraqi oil operations, the US says. Coalition air strikes against tankers and refineries controlled by Isis have merely dented – rather than halted – these exports, it adds.

The militants control around half a dozen oil-producing oilfields. They were quickly able to make them operational and then tapped into established trading networks across northern Iraq, where smuggling has been a fact of life for years. From early July until late October, most of this oil went to Iraqi Kurdistan. The self-proclaimed Islamic caliphate sold oil to Kurdish traders at a major discount. From Kurdistan, the oil was resold to Turkish and Iranian traders.

The amount of oil being produced by ISIS is much lower than what was produced by the Iraqi government. But there is no question that oil production remains a key component of ISIS financial strength and its ability to pay fighters, recruit professionals including doctors, engineers and computer technicians, and to pay for at least some basic services in the areas it controls.

And in Iraq as well as in Syria, the ISIS-controlled oil business involves lots of other parties, including those who are fighting ISIS. Kurdish traders are known to be buying and selling ISIS oil in an illegal but widely acknowledged trading system. According to *The Guardian*, 'One Kurdish parliamentarian admitted it hadn't been shut down altogether. "I would say the illegal trade has decreased by 50 per cent. We have detained several people who were involved in buying oil from Da'esh [ISIS]. The same people provided ISIS with petrol and over 250 pick-up trucks," Mahmoud Haji Omar said. He added that even Shi'a militias fighting the extremists had profited from the trade by taxing oil tankers passing through territory they control.'

Oil could also emerge as a source of diplomatic pressure in the context of the regional and global powers' engagement in the Syrian civil war. But that depends on developments in the global oil business. Many of those powers supporting various sides in Syria – Russia, the US, Saudi Arabia, Iran, Iraq and more – are major oil producers who were seriously affected by the collapse of world oil prices that began in 2014. Russia and Iran, in particular, each a major oil producer highly dependent on oil exports as a large segment of its economy, faced severe consequences as its oil brought in rapidly diminishing amounts of hard currency from the global market.

Despite its similar dependence on oil exports, Saudi Arabia, still the largest Middle East oil exporter, could weather the price crisis much better because of its billions of dollars of oil wealth invested around the world. The Saudis are the dominant force in OPEC, the powerful global oil cartel, which largely allowed the precipitous price drop to happen without cutting production. Such a cut in supply would have had the immediate impact of a price rise – but the Saudis resisted that decision. Many analysts see the Saudi decision rooted in the kingdom's efforts to maintain control of its large global market share – something that it could lose if the practice of hydraulic fracturing, known as fracking, for instance, continues to increase production in the US. With the price of oil remaining low, the thinking goes, fracking becomes less viable (because it's really expensive to produce oil that way – aside from environmental consequences, fracking only makes sense financially if oil prices stay high). So if the amount of fracking-produced oil is reduced, Saudi Arabia keeps a bigger share of the market. The Saudi economy may be hurt by the lower prices, but Saudi wealth means it can survive much better than Russia or Iran.

That gives the Saudi monarchy a great opportunity to pressure Russia. And beginning in early 2015 reports surfaced that exactly that kind of a campaign was under way. As the *New York Times* described it: 'Saudi Arabia has been trying to pressure President Vladimir V Putin of Russia to abandon his support for President Bashar al-Assad of Syria, using its dominance of the global oil markets at a time when the Russian government is reeling from the effects of plummeting oil prices... Any weakening of Russian support for Mr Assad could be one of the first signs that the recent tumult in the oil market is having an impact on global statecraft. Saudi officials... believe that there could be ancillary diplomatic benefits to the country's current strategy of allowing oil prices to stay low – including a chance to negotiate an exit for Mr Assad.'

Given Russia's longstanding support for Syria, particularly its provision of weapons and other military assistance, such a move could prove powerful. US support for such a Russian move, however, would be politically complicated. A rise in global oil prices would be good for the US oil industry and good for the companies involved in environment-destroying fracking. But the other consequence of a successful Saudi-Russian oil-for-Assad deal would be a significant rise in oil prices in the US, which would have a huge impact on US consumers and virtually all of the non-energy sectors of the economy. Outside the US, while a major reduction in Russian support for Assad would have serious consequences on the Syrian government, Iranian support would be unlikely to change – and Iran would also benefit from higher oil prices. For the US, fighting the 'global war on terror' means once again fighting wars at least partly over oil.

What do the Kurds have to do with the current war in Iraq and Syria?

The mobilization against ISIS has pushed Kurdish military forces to the centre of global attention. The Obama administration's return to direct military engagement in Iraq started in 2014 with airstrikes in and around Kobane, although the official *peshmerga*, or Kurdish militia in the autonomous Kurdish region of Iraq, were the main players in reclaiming Kobane from ISIS. The US identifies the Kurds as its most reliable military ally and co-ordinates airstrikes with Kurdish forces. And the Kurds have taken advantage of their newly recognized centrality, including by seizing control of the long-contested oil-rich Iraqi city of Kirkuk outside the official borders of the Kurdish region, to launch new campaigns for recognition, greater autonomy and perhaps independence.

The crisis created by ISIS's conquest of territory across Syria and Iraq has further destabilized already shaky national unity in both countries. Much attention has focused on the Sunni-Shi'a divide, with many Sunnis, especially in Iraq, backing ISIS (reluctantly or not) as protection against the ravages of a sectarian, Shi'a-dominated government in Baghdad.

And with both Iraq and Syria already seriously divided along sectarian and ethnic lines, that religious split continues to undermine the existence of the nations themselves. In both countries, however, the ISIS crisis has created new opportunities as well as new challenges for Kurdish populations and their longstanding efforts to win at least greater autonomy, if not full-scale independence.

At the beginning of the civil war in Syria, the Kurds were able to manoeuvre into a position in which they could consolidate a higher level of autonomy, and the regime in Damascus mostly did not target them. While many Kurds remained strong critics of the government's repression, they mostly played a minor role in the Syrian opposition movements. In the summer of 2012 the Syrian military largely pulled out of several large Kurdish towns. Tensions between the Syrian Kurdish forces and Syrian rebels rose, and in 2012 near Aleppo and later in other areas there were direct clashes between militias of the US and Western-backed Free Syrian Army and the multi-party Kurdish People's Defence Unit (YPG) militias.

As *Time* magazine described it: 'Even if they oppose Assad, many Kurds, particularly those aligned with the PYD [one of the most influential Syrian Kurdish parties], see the rebels as Islamist thugs acting on behalf of neighboring Turkey to control a post-Assad Syria. Many insurgents, meanwhile, resent the PYD and its armed supporters for staying out of the war against Assad, accusing it of being a cat's paw for the regime.' While that may be somewhat overstated, it does give a good flavour of the contradictions between the sides. For the US, the tension is further complicated by the fact that the PYD is allied with the PKK, the Kurdish Workers Party, in Turkey, which has long been included on the US anti-terrorism list even while its leaders were negotiating with Ankara.

The situation in Turkey became further complicated in 2015, in the run-up to new elections. Political unease in the country was rising, Kurdish-Turkish tensions rose, and Turkish leaders, especially President Erdogan, were widely seen as using anti-Kurdish sentiments to build nationalist support in the election. The November 2015 vote brought Erdogan's Islamist-oriented AKP back to power again, and the two-year-old Turkey-PKK ceasefire collapsed. Attacks on supporters of the Kurdish-leftist HDP party increased, with a brutal bombing of a largely

Kurdish peace rally in Ankara in October 2015 leaving more than 100 activists dead. The attack was widely blamed on ISIS supporters, but the government was held responsible for allowing too-easy transit over the Turkey-Syria border for ISIS militants and supporters.

In Iraq, the divide between Kurds, who dominate the northern sector of the country including key oilfields, and both the Shi'a-dominated government and Sunni-led rebel forces escalated throughout the years of US-imposed economic sanctions (1990-2003) and the US invasion and occupation (2003-11) and continued after US troops were withdrawn. One of the key points of dispute was the city of Kirkuk – outside the official border of the Kurdish regional government's authority. Control of this mixed Kurdish-Arab-Turkoman city was, and is, an oil prize. Both the government in Baghdad and the Kurdish regional government had claimed the city.

In 2014, the success of ISIS in capturing territory in Iraq, and the resulting collapse of the Iraqi military in those regions, led to an unexpected opportunity for the Kurds, who were able to seize and maintain control of Kirkuk while Baghdad, its fractured military, its US and regional backers, and the world's press were focused solely on land grabs by ISIS. The Kurdish seizure of Kirkuk, with all its oil facilities, remained under the radar.

Kurdish fighters re-emerged as key players in the escalating ISIS crisis in August 2014, when ISIS forces overran the largely Kurdish community in Sinjar, in Iraq near the Syrian border. Tens of thousands of the mainly Yazidi residents fled their town to seek refuge on nearby Mount Sinjar. It was the Kurdish YPG, supported at the end by soldiers of the peshmerga – the militia of the officially recognized Kurdish regional authority in Iraq – who played the major role in saving the Yazidis (mainly Kurdish themselves) from their desperate situation trapped on top of the mountain. (See 'How did the US justify its return of troops to Syria and Iraq').

The fighting in Kobane, the largely Syrian Kurdish

town on the Turkish border, erupted in October 2014 when ISIS threatened to occupy the city. Kobane was not strategically important, but because Kobane was so close to the Turkish border, where international journalists could see the fighting, it quickly became emblematic of Kurdish identity, as well as of the failure of the US strategy to protect the civilian population and the refusal of the Turkish military (including soldiers based just across the border within view of Kobane) to intervene.

Facing domestic and international 'Twitter factor' pressure, the US launched a few airstrikes against ISIS around Kobane and eventually persuaded Turkey to allow a few carefully vetted units of the peshmerga to cross the border from Iraq to help defend the city. But in the midst of the Kobane crisis Secretary of State John Kerry announced: 'Kobane does not define the strategy for the coalition in respect to Da'esh [ISIS]. Kobane is one community and it is a tragedy what is happening there. And we do not diminish that. But we have said from day one that it is going to take a period of time to bring the coalition thoroughly to the table to rebuild some of the morale and capacity of the Iraqi army. And to begin the focus of where we ought to be focusing first, which is in Iraq. That is the current strategy.' For the US, ensuring that ISIS did not take over oil-rich and strategically important Iraq was the issue – not the plight of Kurdish civilians in Syria.

The increasingly visible role of Kurdish fighters, both in Syria and Iraq, and particularly with the emergence of Rojava, in northern Syria as a largely autonomous Kurdish enclave, forced long-simmering Kurdish demands for greater autonomy and perhaps independence to the top of US and regional strategic considerations. Even allowing the peshmerga to participate in protecting the population of Kobane was fraught with complications. The US urgently wanted more local involvement on the ground, while its NATO ally Turkey remained adamant that the Iraqi Kurdish forces not be allowed to play a leading role, for fear that it would encourage greater demands for autonomy for Turkey's Kurds.

After months of fighting, ISIS was routed from Kobane, but by then the population had mostly fled and the town had been virtually destroyed. In February 2015 a BBC correspondent able to enter Kobane reported: 'Kurdish fighters are now consolidating their hold over the town. But driving the IS [ISIS] from here came at tremendous cost. Hundreds of coalition airstrikes have flattened most of the town.'

But it was not the airstrikes that had beaten back ISIS. The *Washington Post* headline in late January 2015 read: 'Kurds Drive Islamic State Fighters from Strategic Town of Kobane'. Importantly for Kobane residents, credit for liberating their town had gone to Kurdish fighters, not to the US and its coalition allies. Talking to a BBC reporter, the 12-year-old granddaughter of one of the small number of Kobane residents who remained throughout the fighting said: 'Kurdish officials didn't abandon us. We are going to school now. And we are very happy because we will be able to go back to our villages. They liberated our lands,' she added proudly.

What role is the United Nations playing, and what more is needed?

During the early years of the first global war on terror, the George Bush-Tony Blair axis worked very hard to exclude the UN from any significant role. Within 24 hours of the 9/11 attacks, the Bush administration proposed a UN Security Council resolution that passed unanimously with enormous fervour, expressing sympathy and condolences to Americans and 'unequivocally condemning' the terrorist acts. The Council called on all countries to 'work together' to bring those responsible to justice, and agreed on 'increased co-operation and full implementation of the relevant international anti-terrorist conventions and Security Council resolutions.'

What the Security Council did not do was authorize war – the resolution was not passed under the terms of Chapter VII, the one part of the UN Charter through which the Council can authorize the use of military force. It was not a situation in which Washington feared that a stronger resolution might not pass – it was clear anything proposed on that day, while the twin towers still smouldered and many UN diplomats and their families still faced the trauma of having been in the vicinity of the attack, that anything the US wanted, the US would get. The limited text reflected a deliberate decision by the Bush administration not to allow the United Nations to be in any kind of decision-making position.

In the run-up to the 2003 invasion of Iraq, Bush and Blair tried desperately to win Security Council approval for the war. But by that time a massive global peace movement had mobilized, putting unprecedented pressure on countries around the world. Europe split, and smaller, weaker, poorer countries that would ordinarily have quickly succumbed to US pressure stood firm against the call to war. For eight months, the United Nations did what its charter requires, but what it is too rarely allowed to do: stop the scourge of war. The US-UK invasion and occupation were not only illegitimate, immoral and based on lies; under international law, they were also absolutely illegal.

Technically that changed in May 2003 when the UN's resistance collapsed and the Security Council passed a resolution endorsing the occupation and agreeing to collaborate with it. That decision, despite the predominantly humanitarian nature of the UN's actual work at that time, set the stage directly for the horrific suicide truck-bomb attack on the UN's Baghdad headquarters in August 2003, killing at least 22 people, of whom 16 were UN staff.

While it remained in the war-torn region in following years, working primarily to provide humanitarian assistance to occupation-devastated populations and on occasion sending special envoys to crisis zones, the UN did not emerge as a major political player in the war on terror again until the Libya crisis broke.

In March 2011, permanent Security Council members Britain and France began a campaign for a military assault, starting with a no-fly zone in Libya. The US initially rejected the initiative because influential forces within the Obama administration, the Pentagon, Congress, and other US elites believed a no-fly zone would not protect civilians and, more important, would pull the US into a quagmire with no clear exit strategy or basis to declare 'victory'. But, after a few days of internal debate, the pro-intervention forces, largely based in Hillary Clinton's State Department, won the day. The US then told the British and the French that they could not support the existing no-fly zone plan, but that instead of simply vetoing the proposed resolution, they would redraft it to fit US requirements.

The result was a vastly expanded resolution that not only endorsed a no-fly zone but also authorized 'all necessary measures' to be used in the name of protecting civilians. The language legalized unlimited military force, and because 'to protect civilians' was not defined, it was left to the US-NATO coalition forces themselves to decide how far they wanted to go.

The Security Council reached a very unusual near-consensus on approving the assault on Libya. The debate focused on the need to protect civilians, and indeed the text of the resolution started with the call for 'the immediate establishment of a ceasefire and... the need to intensify efforts to find a solution to the crisis which responds to the legitimate demands of the Libyan people'. It took note of the goal of 'facilitating dialogue to lead to the political reforms necessary to find a peaceful and sustainable solution'. But it was widely believed, at least outside the Security Council itself, that US-NATO intervention would never be limited to humanitarian efforts, and that regime change was certainly on the table.

That turned out to be true. A no-fly zone, attacks on Libyan leader Muammar al-Qadafi's military, and escalating civilian casualties ensued. The Security Council resolution's language of using 'all necessary means' quickly shifted from protecting civilians to open calls for regime change. It was never fully clear why countries such as South Africa gave in to the West's pressure campaign, nor why Russian and Chinese veto power was never asserted. South Africa's vote supporting the resolution appears to be the reason for an African Union delegation being turned away at Libya's border, where the group hoped to enter to begin some kind of negotiations.

A ceasefire didn't seem to be at the top of anyone's agenda, and certainly not that of the UN's most powerful members. The UN, having provided legality (if not legitimacy – it took Arab League and African Union endorsement for that) to the NATO-US air war against Libya, had little further role to play. And three months later the head of South Africa's Ministry of Foreign Affairs admitted his country now 'regretted' having voted for the no-fly zone.

At the core of the debates over Libya was the UN's concept of 'responsibility to protect', the idea that when people face repression or worse from their own government, the international community has the obligation to step in, relying first on non-military means and only turning to military solutions as the last resort. But for Libya, it would have been far easier to accept the claimed necessity of US-UK-French-NATO military intervention in Libya as being based on humanitarian motives if *non-military* but active intervention had already been under way in similar (if smaller) crises.

For example, if the US had immediately cut all military and economic aid to Bahrain at the first sign that its king was bringing foreign troops in to suppress the uprising. If the US had immediately ended all arms sales and stopped the current weapons pipeline to Saudi

Arabia when its soldiers crossed Bahrain's causeway. If the US had announced a complete halt in all military aid to Yemen when then-President Abdullah Ali Saleh's forces first attacked the demonstrators. Not to mention the possibility of a decision to cut military aid to Israel and end the decades of US-guaranteed impunity for war crimes. All of those actions were possible, appropriate, non-military and would have had huge humanitarian impacts. When none of them was even attempted, it was difficult to accept the claim that military intervention in Libya was really grounded in humanitarian motives.

The UN was next called upon to respond to the rapidly escalating civil war in Syria. One of the first moves was by the UN's Human Rights Council, which voted to send a fact-finding mission in April 2011, soon after the crisis erupted. Later efforts to send investigation teams were mainly met by the refusal of the Syrian government to allow them access. In the first months of the crisis, as the Assad regime's military response to the unarmed political opposition morphed into a widening civil war, the Security Council took up the issue. Unable to reach agreement on a resolution, the Council's first move was to issue a statement urging the Syrian regime to comply with human rights norms, calling on all sides to stop the violence, and supporting a Syrian political process to end the crisis. Statements of concern, condemnations of the violence, and demands for ending the political repression and allowing humanitarian assistance continued to be issued by the UN Secretary-General, the Human Rights Council and other agencies of the organization.

The Security Council continued to debate the Syria question, but the wide gap between the two groups of permanent members – the US, UK and France versus Russia and China – made agreement on a resolution very difficult. The first to come to a vote, on 4 February 2012, resulted in vetoes by Russia and China, based on the resolution's support for an earlier Arab League plan requiring Assad to step down. It included broader language condemning violence on all sides, but Moscow and Beijing were not prepared to accept the call for Assad to resign and hand power to a deputy. The following day, US Secretary of State Hillary Clinton called for the formation of a 'Friends of Democratic Syria' coalition outside the UN.

Soon after the Security Council resolution was vetoed, the General Assembly passed a similar resolution based on the Arab League plan, rather than using the opportunity to craft a different approach to demand an end to violence and a new diplomatic initiative.

Two later Security Council efforts also resulted in vetoes, but in both cases the draft resolutions were rooted in Chapter VII of the UN Charter, which permits sanctions but can also be used to authorize military action. In July 2012, when the second veto of a Chapter VII resolution took place, *The Guardian* quoted the British ambassador claiming that Security Council members had 'offered flexibility on Russia and China's concerns', and that therefore it was 'irrational' that those two countries 'argued that a Chapter VII resolution is somehow designed to seek conflict through the backdoor'. According to *The Guardian*, US Ambassador Susan Rice said that 'the suggestion that the resolution would give the green light for foreign forces to enter Syria was "paranoid if not disingenuous",' and that the resolution 'would in no way authorise or even pave the way for foreign military intervention'. The following day, not long after that resolution was vetoed, the foreign military intervention began on all sides – leading, most recently, to the direct military engagement of US warplanes and missiles in Syria, as well as the US, Britain and their regional allies arming, training and funding Syrian as well as foreign fighters.

The next UN move was the appointment in late February 2012, jointly with the Arab League, of former Secretary-General Kofi Annan as the special envoy to Syria – tasked with engaging with all sides inside and outside Syria to end the violence and promote a peaceful resolution. In mid-March Annan submitted his six-point peace plan to the Security Council.

The plan called for the following:

- Syrian-led political process to address the legitimate aspirations and concerns of the Syrian people
- a commitment to stop the fighting and respect a UN-supervised ceasefire by both the government and the opposition
- timely humanitarian assistance, including the implementation of a daily two-hour humanitarian pause
- release of arbitrarily detained persons, especially the most vulnerable, and political prisoners
- access and freedom of movement for journalists
- respect for the freedom of association and the right to peacefully demonstrate.

The Syrian government accepted the plan on 27 March and a ceasefire as called for in the plan was announced on 12 April 2012, to be verified by a Security Council-mandated observer team. But the ceasefire was never implemented.

In March 2012 the UN's High Commissioner for Human Rights Navi Pillay cautioned against arming the Syrian opposition, stating that it threatened to escalate the violence. She was right – the additional arms flooding into both secular and most especially rising extremist forces in Syria, smuggled over the border from Iraq, accessed from newly accessible stockpiles in Libya, and especially provided directly by US allies in the region, all served to escalate the government's repression to full-scale civil war.

By August, Kofi Annan had resigned. It was clear that the special envoy was not even close to achieving a ceasefire, the starting point of his six-point peace plan, and prospects were looking dimmer than ever. But his resignation reflected two other stark realities. First, outside players – most especially the US, Saudi Arabia, Qatar, Turkey, Jordan, the UAE, Russia and Iran – were operating solely for their own narrow strategic interests, not on behalf of the Syrian people. Second, the UN Security Council and its member states provided no real support for any potential political solution that might actually work. Instead, they acted to strengthen the military forces on both sides.

It was significant that Annan directly criticized the Council and its members, especially the five permanent members – Britain, China, France, Russia and the US – known as the Permanent Five. While the Council had endorsed the Annan plan early on, there was never any real support for it or for the work of the UN observer team in Syria. The three US-British-French resolutions on Syria called for harsh UN sanctions and a range of other economic and diplomatic pressures on the regime of Bashar al-Assad. They were all vetoed by Russia and China. The US and its allies had maintained (perhaps even truthfully at that pre-ISIS moment) that direct engagement in the military battle against the Syrian government was not their intention. But two of the three vetoed resolutions would have been taken under Chapter VII of the UN Charter – the same precondition required for the use of force.

The resolutions might well have set the political stage to legalize what would later occur anyway: direct US/European/NATO participation in the fighting. Looking at the precedent of the Security Council vote on Libya the year before, when the Council-authorized no-fly zone was immediately transformed into an all-out US/NATO air war, that kind of escalation was certainly a reasonable assumption. Further negotiations might well have rendered Security Council agreement on a resolution possible. Perhaps Russia and China might have accepted resolutions calling for pressure, even an arms embargo (prohibiting sales, assistance, repairs, or anything else) to both sides – if the resolution was not based on Chapter VII. But that proposal was not forthcoming, and instead the Council remained paralysed.

When Special Envoy Kofi Annan resigned in early August 2012, it was clear that outside forces were not willing to impose enough pressure on their Syrian allies to make a ceasefire, an arms embargo, a new diplomatic initiative, or other necessary components of a peace process possible. He stated that 'increasing militarization on the ground and the clear lack of unity in the Security Council have fundamentally changed the circumstances for the effective exercise of my role'. He went on to add: 'The bloodshed continues, most of all because of the Syrian government's intransigence and continuing refusal to implement the six-point plan, and also because of the escalating military campaign of the opposition, all of which is compounded by the disunity of the international community. At a time when we need – when the Syrian people desperately need action, there continues to be finger-pointing and name-calling in the Security Council.'

A few weeks later the Council appointed veteran Algerian diplomat and international civil servant Lakhdar Brahimi to replace Annan as the joint special envoy. But as the war in Syria continued to escalate, he would have no more success than his predecessor. One of his first efforts, a ceasefire in October in honour of the Muslim holiday of Eid al-Adha, failed to achieve its goal.

In August 2013 the United Nations Security Council became the main venue where the debate on how to respond to the chemical weapons attack outside of Damascus went forward. (See 'What was the story behind the chemical weapons attack?') But the role of the global institution was sidelined relative to the debate in the US, Britain, and NATO regarding possible military responses.

Following the chemical weapons crisis, Brahimi turned to convening a major conference on Syria as the cornerstone of his work as special envoy. The UN acted as convener for the January 2014 'Geneva II' conference, an attempt to bring together key Syrian parties from both the government and the opposition. But the conference never succeeded, chiefly due to Washington's refusal to allow Iran to be invited, despite, or perhaps because of, the fact that Iran was a major player in the Syrian war. Recognizing that diplomacy that leaves out major players can never succeed, UN Secretary General Ban Ki-moon invited Tehran to participate. But after 24 hours of intense US pressure, he 'disinvited' Iran's representatives. Negotiations went on for two weeks but failed to reach any agreement on ending the war or even temporary ceasefires or humanitarian corridors.

In May 2014 Brahimi resigned, expressing his 'apologies once more that we haven't been able to help [the Syrian people] as much as they deserve, as much as we should have, and also to tell them that the tragedy in their country shall be solved... they have shown incredible resilience and dignity.'

As political efforts floundered, the UN's greatest concern was the escalating humanitarian crisis. The UN agencies for children, refugees, food and health all moved into crisis mode to respond, but lack of sufficient financial support from UN member states meant that their work, while vitally important for the very survival of millions of Syrian refugees and displaced, was rarely sufficient.

Ironically, the great divide between the two groups of permanent members of the Security Council – the US, Britain, and France versus Russia and China – may have actually enabled the Council to abide by its UN Charter obligation to prevent the 'scourge of war' from spreading even further. While a resolution focusing on a mutual ceasefire, arms embargo and renewed political negotiations would have been important, it was clear that the US and its allies would never have allowed that without Chapter VII authorization and some reference to Assad stepping down. It remains unclear whether Russia and China might have supported such a resolution without those two deal-breakers. But certainly, if the two sides *had* agreed on a Chapter VII resolution, there would have been an even greater level of escalation and violence, and even less of a chance of bringing a quick end to the war.

There is a kind of revisionist history of the UN popularized by some in the US and elsewhere, which claims that the UN fails when it refuses to endorse US, NATO, 'Western' wars. During the 'humanitarian interventions' of the 1990s and the Iraq War of 2003, the UN was excoriated as a failure when it *rejected* participation in military action, rather than being recognized as a failure when it *joined* the war train. But the reality is quite the opposite. In fact one of the greatest achievements of the UN was the refusal of the Security Council to endorse George W Bush's war on Iraq. The eight months of UN resistance in 2002-03 brought the global institution into partnership with many governments and, more important, with the extraordinary global peace movement of that period – the moment when 'the world said no to war'. That should be a moment to reclaim, not to reject.

Obama planned to withdraw almost all US troops from Afghanistan by 2017 – why did he change his mind?

When Barack Obama was elected he promised to end what he called the 'dumb war' in Iraq, but also to escalate the war in Afghanistan, which he promptly did. He sent an additional 47,000 US troops to Afghanistan in his first year in office, but made clear his intention to withdraw almost all US troops by the end of 2014. In mid-2010, Obama's second year in office, the total number of al-Qaeda fighters left in Afghanistan, according to then-CIA Director Leon Panetta, was '50 to 100, maybe less'. But there were still almost 100,000 US troops occupying the country.

As al-Qaeda shifted its fighters to Pakistan, al-Qaeda affiliates sprang up in new venues across the region.

Once again, US ground troops, air force pilots and armed drones proved the limits of military force in defeating terrorism. Public support in the US was dropping rapidly, but support from the Pentagon stayed firm.

Many al-Qaeda and other fighters whom the US identified as 'terrorists' were in fact killed in the US war. It was never clear exactly how many, because the Pentagon early on said 'We don't do body counts' and had no decent means of determining identities of the casualties of airstrikes. It was later revealed that all males of military age killed by US bombs or drones were automatically classified as militants. What was certain was that many civilians were killed. In 2006 other agencies did begin some effort at counting civilian casualties – through 2013 that seven-year casualty estimate was about 18,700 Afghan civilians dead. According to the UN, 2014 saw the highest number of civilian casualties yet, and in August 2015 the UN Assistance Mission in Afghanistan reported that 2015 was on track to match or exceed those already high figures.

The US explained the escalation of fighting in Afghanistan in rather convoluted terms as a way of speeding up an end to the US role in the war. In his January 2014 State of the Union address, Obama did mention one substantive change – that 'while our relationship with Afghanistan will change, one thing will not: our resolve that terrorists do not launch attacks against our country.' So that was the real shift. Now it was official that the US would continue occupying Afghanistan solely to defend US interests. It no longer had anything to do with protecting Afghans.

In May 2014 Obama announced a plan to withdraw most US troops and end their combat role in Afghanistan by the end of that year, leaving behind almost 10,000 troops until the end of 2016.

The US gradually reduced troop numbers, but by early December 2014 the White House announced another change, adding 1,000 more troops to remain in Afghanistan, for a total of almost 11,000, and an anticipated new US-NATO mission to begin some time in 2015. That new deployment would include 12,000 more US and NATO troops primarily focused on training the Afghan military, while some unknown thousands of US counter-terrorism troops would continue operating in Afghanistan, still ostensibly against al-Qaeda. (No-one at the press conferences asked President Obama or then-Secretary of Defense Chuck Hagel if the number of al-Qaeda operatives in Afghanistan was still '50 to 100, maybe less' as Panetta had stated.)

In late November 2014 Hagel resigned. The White House claimed his departure did not indicate any change in strategy. But he had been brought in to oversee the withdrawal of troops and the ending of the Iraq and Afghanistan wars, and those wars were now escalating instead – more troops were being kept on a longer mission in Afghanistan, and US troops had returned to fight in Iraq. Hagel had essentially already ceded leadership of the Pentagon to General Martin Dempsey, then-Chair of the Joint Chiefs of Staff, who had been urging a much more aggressive military posture both in Afghanistan and Iraq.

Ashton Carter, the Pentagon insider who replaced Hagel as Secretary of Defense, travelled to Afghanistan just days after being confirmed. When he returned, new evidence of mission creep emerged. On 22 February 2015 a National Public Radio host introduced Carter with the words, 'When it comes to Afghanistan, the line out of the White House has been clear and consistent. US combat operations are over. US troops are coming home. And the Afghans are in charge. But this weekend, the new US Secretary of Defense flew to Kabul and said that might not be the case.'

The US and Britain promised they would not abandon Afghanistan after Western combat troops were withdrawn. But no new money was pledged, and it remained unclear just what that 'support' would look like other than keeping US and NATO troops in the country longer than planned.

That decision partly reflected the continuation of the Afghanistan civil war, which was escalating despite the reductions in US and NATO troops and despite the fact that the vast majority of al-Qaeda operatives were gone.

The Taliban, another extremist Islamist organization, had won Afghanistan's civil war in 1996, then ruled the country until it was overthrown by the US invasion of October 2001. The US then replaced the Taliban with a government made up of their longtime opponents, known as the Northern Alliance (many of whose leaders were just as extremist, misogynistic and violent as the Taliban). This set the stage for a continuation of Afghanistan's longstanding civil war, fought by the Taliban and other insurgent forces against the US-backed Afghan government plus a host of pro-government but largely unaccountable militias. The revived conflict continued to create escalating numbers of civilian casualties. Almost 15 years later, the Taliban continued to fight even as the US and UK gradually withdrew most troops.

The civil war also provided a pretext for continuing US military engagement in the country, despite the acknowledgement that al-Qaeda, the original ostensible target of the US 'global war on terror' in Afghanistan, was long gone. Early in 2014, when it was still unclear whether the government in Kabul would sign a security agreement with the US, top Pentagon officials made clear that they wanted to keep troops and continue fighting in Afghanistan. While some referred to threats of a serious attack against Kabul and the potential collapse of the US-backed government, the main point of reference was the possibility that Afghanistan could again be used as a base for international terrorism – the expressed concern was for US interests, not for the people of Afghanistan.

In February 2015, Ashton Carter, the new Secretary of Defense, dismissed reports that some elements in Afghanistan were linking themselves to ISIS, saying they appeared to be just extremists 'rebranding' themselves. 'The reports I've seen still have them in small numbers,' he told reporters on his way home from Afghanistan.

Yet those small numbers, whether of al-Qaeda or ISIS in Afghanistan, seemingly kept the US-backed Afghan military from defeating them. During 2014 more than 5,000 members of the Afghan security forces were killed, the highest yearly toll yet. In December that year the *New York Times* cited outgoing commander of the US forces in Afghanistan, Lieutenant-General Joseph Anderson, who spoke to them after the ceremonies marking the end of the US combat mission. '"The record casualties of Afghan forces are not sustainable, and neither are their astounding desertion rates," he said. "Political meddling, not intelligence, drives Afghan military missions..." It was a reflection on the mission that was in stark contrast to the unbridled renditions of success offered during the ceremony by commanders, including General Anderson.' And unsurprisingly, six months later the *New York Times* acknowledged that 2015 was 'already shaping up to be worse for the Afghan Army and the national police.'

Anderson's claims were also in stark contrast to the idea that somehow more years of US/NATO 'training' of Afghan security forces with little or no loyalty to the US/NATO-created central government in Kabul, and more years of US-backed war, was going to do anything to end the Taliban attacks or help build better lives for the Afghan people – let alone win the global war on terror.

The US had yet to win that war – and more military engagement was unlikely to change that reality. A November 2014 poll indicated that despite many Afghans saying they would like to see a greater US commitment to Afghanistan, support for the Taliban had doubled from 2010 to 20 per cent of Afghans. Some 31 per cent supported the presence of foreign jihadist fighters – also higher than 2010. Once again, military force fails to change people's hearts and minds.

What was the significance of the US bombing of the Doctors Without Borders hospital in Afghanistan?

On 3 October 2015, US bombers attacked a well-lit, well-known, well-marked trauma hospital run by Doctors Without Borders (MSF) in Kunduz, Afghanistan. At least 30 were killed, including medical staff and patients, three of them children. Hundreds were injured. The MSF staff had provided exact GPS coordinates to both US and Afghan military authorities just four days earlier, and the hospital was, according to the *New York Times*, 'among the most brightly lit buildings in Kunduz on the night a circling American gunship destroyed it.' Throughout the hour-long attack, MSF staff continued to contact US and Afghan military officials, begging them to stop the bombing.

MSF's Head of Programmes in northern Afghanistan, Heman Nagarathnam, described how 'the bombs hit and then we heard the plane circle round. There was a pause, and then more bombs hit. This happened again and again. When I made it out from the office, the main hospital building was engulfed in flames. Those people that could had moved quickly to the building's two bunkers to seek safety. But patients who were unable to escape burned to death as they lay in their beds.'

The US first claimed it had launched an air strike at 2.15am that Saturday morning against 'individuals threatening the force', and that 'the strike may have resulted in collateral damage to a nearby medical facility'. Then the US explanations began to change, rotating through at least four different stories: bombing the hospital was a mistake; the bombing was to support US forces under fire; US forces bombed the hospital to back up Afghan troops under fire; the hospital was attacked because it was under Taliban control. Surviving MSF staff on the ground made clear the Taliban was not in control of the hospital, that their rule prohibiting any weapons in the hospital was intact, that there was no fighting in the gardens surrounding the hospital buildings. President Obama officially apologized for the attack, but rejected MSF's demand for an independent international investigation, claiming that the Pentagon's own investigation of itself was sufficient.

Under the Geneva Conventions, attacking a hospital is virtually always a war crime. The UN's High Commissioner for Human Rights, Zeid Ra'ad al Hussein, described the bombing as 'utterly tragic, inexcusable, and possibly even criminal. International and Afghan military planners have an obligation to respect and protect civilians at all times, and medical facilities and personnel are the object of a special protection. These obligations apply no matter whose air force is involved, and irrespective of the location.'

In MSF's own report, issued just weeks after the bombing, the staff on the ground confirmed there were no weapons or fighting in the hospital compound before the bombing began. The day before the bombing attack, an unnamed US official in Washington had asked MSF if Taliban fighters were 'holed up' in the hospital. MSF confirmed the hospital was filled with patients who included wounded government and Taliban fighters – in keeping with their longstanding commitment to treating all injured people, regardless of who they are or what side they had been fighting for. International law also recognizes that the wounded, especially in a hospital, are no longer considered combatants. The MSF report also noted that staff members trying to flee hospital buildings in the compound were shot at from the air while the US planes were dropping bombs.

Three days after his forces bombed the MSF hospital, the head of US troops in Afghanistan, General John Campbell, testified that US troops might need to stay in Afghanistan longer because the Afghan military needed support. 'Strategic patience' would be required, he said – but by Congress and the US public, not by Afghans. Just over a week later, while still refusing to co-operate with an independent investigation of the hospital bombing, the Obama administration announced it was indeed reversing the President's earlier commitment to withdraw all troops from Afghanistan by the end of 2016. The lesson of the US bombing of an Afghan hospital and killing its doctors and patients appeared to be that US forces should remain to fight in Afghanistan indefinitely.

What does all of this have to do with Palestine and Israel?

The new war on terror – meaning the war against ISIS, the civil war in Syria, the return of US troops to war in Iraq, the escalating drone war, and more – is not being directly fought in or by Palestine or Israel, Palestinians or Israelis. But that does not mean there is no connection. On the contrary, there are on-the-ground, political, regional/strategic and ideological links.

While Palestinians inside Israel and the occupied territories are not directly affected, Palestinian refugees in and around Syria are facing serious war-related problems. The greatest crisis confronts the Palestinians who lived in refugee camps in Syria, most of them in and around Damascus. Those families included Palestinians who fled to Syria during the *nakba*, or catastrophe, the massive forced expulsion and dispossession of Palestinians from their land during the 1947-48 war of Israeli independence. Others were living in Syria after having been made refugees for the second, third, or even more times – some who escaped the *nakba* into the West Bank, perhaps, and then were forced out in 1967, ending up in Jordan. Maybe they were living in a refugee camp in Jordan and were expelled in 1970 during Jordan's anti-Palestinian campaigns. Maybe they ended up in one of the numerous Palestinian refugee camps in Lebanon and were expelled from there during the Israeli invasion and occupation of 1982.

With the outbreak of Syria's civil war, hundreds of thousands of Palestinian refugees still living in camps in Syria faced dire threats. Early in the Syrian crisis most Palestinians tried to avoid taking sides, fearing the consequences. But as the popular uprising shifted to a lethal, multi-faceted civil war, the situation became much worse. In July 2012 the UN agency responsible for providing basic survival services to Palestinian refugees, UNRWA, issued a statement of direct concern, particularly for the more than 100,000 refugees living in Yarmouk camp in Damascus.

'UNRWA views with increasingly grave concern the situation in Syria, particularly as regards the implications for the stability and protection of 500,000 Palestine refugees across the country,' the agency said. 'The current situation in the Damascus neighborhood of Yarmouk and in rural Damascus, home to both Syrian and Palestinian communities, is especially worrying.'

UNRWA pushed all sides of the conflict to work 'to preserve human life, to avoid forced displacement and to exercise the utmost restraint' and to demonstrate 'respect for the neutrality and integrity of UN installations' and places where refugees and other civilians live. 'UNRWA has appealed to the Syrian authorities to safeguard the security of Palestine refugees wherever they reside in Syria.'

But safeguarding the security of refugees was not on the agenda of the Syrian military, nor was it a priority for any of the myriad opposition forces. Many thousands of Palestinian refugees in Yarmouk and elsewhere in Syria were forced to flee their homes once again. Israel continued its post-1948 denial of the refugees' international-law-granted right of return to their homes, forcing many to seek refuge in already overcrowded refugee camps in Lebanon and Jordan, neither of whom were particularly welcoming of the newest refugee population.

In December 2012 Syrian military jets bombed areas of Damascus, including Yarmouk, hitting a mosque and a school inside the camp. The already-severe humanitarian crisis in the camp turned dire. A photograph, which unexpectedly went viral around the world and was the basis for a #SaveYarmouk Twitter campaign, showed the desperation of the 18,000 Palestinians left in the camp, many of them children and elderly people, unable to flee.

It was perhaps the bitterest of ironies that many of the Palestinians fleeing Yarmouk who managed to get to Lebanon found refuge, of a sort, in the decrepit Beirut-area refugee camps known as Sabra and Shatila – the site of a brutal 1982 massacre by Lebanese Christian extremists armed and backed by the Israeli military.

The situation in Syria did not improve. By July 2013 the 18,000 Palestinians left in Yarmouk were fully under siege by the Syrian regime, and water was cut off in September 2014, meaning residents had to rely on untreated ground water or open wells, carrying cans of water since there was no electricity to fill tanks.

On 25 February 2015, UNRWA spokesperson Chris Gunness issued the following statement:

UNRWA was unable to distribute assistance in Yarmouk today, 25 February.

UNRWA assesses the security situation in Yarmouk daily and requests relevant authorities to facilitate the distribution of humanitarian assistance to the civilian population. Over the previous two months, Yarmouk and its surrounding areas have seen a serious escalation in armed conflict, including frequent exchanges of fire and the use of heavy weapons, which have persistently disrupted the distribution of life-saving humanitarian aid to the 18,000 civilians trapped in the area. UNRWA remains deeply concerned that no successful distribution has been completed since 6 December 2014.

Approximately 400 food parcels are required each day to meet the minimum food needs of this extremely vulnerable population. In 2014, on days when all concerned actors co-operated fully to give priority to meeting the humanitarian needs of civilians in Yarmouk, UNRWA proved capable of distributing up to 1,000 food parcels per day. To stop the suffering of Yarmouk's civilians, UNRWA calls for this level of co-operation to resume, for the immediate cessation of armed hostilities in and around Yarmouk, and for all concerned parties to act in ways that promote the protection of Yarmouk's civilians and give the utmost priority to their humanitarian needs.

UNRWA had issued the same statement, word for word, every day for almost three months.

Writing in *Electronic Intifada*, Nael Bitarie described his own flight from Yarmouk, where people had once tried to remain neutral in the uprising. 'Our neutrality did not protect us from either Assad's forces or from rebels, however. Not long ago, Yarmouk was the capital of the Palestinian diaspora in Syria. Today, the camp has been destroyed.'

By April 2015 Yarmouk's destruction was virtually complete. While the 18,000 people still inside (3,500 of them children) had already suffered through months of the Syrian government's siege, they now faced ISIS forces who invaded the camp. Fighting escalated, with government and ISIS troops, as well as other militias, turning the camp into a battlefield. According to Gunness, the refugees' 'lives are threatened. They are holed up in their battered homes too terrified to move, which is why we are saying that there must be a pause [in fighting], there must be humanitarian access for groups like UNRWA.'

When a reporter asked why the starving and dying residents of Yarmouk didn't receive global attention until ISIS overran the camp, Gunness replied: 'The question is, can this world attention be translated into political action? Because we have long said that the time for humanitarian action alone has long passed, and what we need is the world powers – the big players – to bring the necessary pressures to bear on the parties on the ground.' As of the end of October 2015, despite some tentative diplomatic moves, no such clear initiative by the world powers was in sight.

Within the broader context of the Syrian civil war, one of the eight separate wars making up the fighting in Syria was the fight between the US and Israel versus Iran. That made Israel a player in the Syrian civil war, although one that was not directly supporting any of the forces fighting on the ground. Israel did intervene directly, bombing Syrian targets, particularly in the non-occupied side of the Golan Heights.

The unevenness of Israel's role reflects the counterintuitive reality that for decades the Syrian regime – led by Bashar al-Assad since 2000 and by his father, Hafez al-Assad since 1970 – had served as an unacknowledged useful neighbour for Israel. Despite Syrian rhetoric about resistance and defending the Palestinians, both Assads were ultimately quite helpful to Israel, most especially by keeping the Israeli-occupied Golan Heights quiet, its population kept under tight control to prevent serious uprisings or resistance.

On the global political side, the renewed US involvement in the Iraq war and the relentless casualties of the Syrian civil war – though covered far less in the media than the up-close-and-personal violence of ISIS – both served as a diversion from the violence of occupation and apartheid that continue to shape Israeli policy and action toward the Palestinians. With the civil war raging inside Syria, Israel was able to attack Syrian positions with little fear of consequences.

Israel had long relied on Syria's backing of Hamas, the Islamist party elected in the Gaza Strip, as the basis for claiming Syria was supporting terrorism. It was a blow to that Israeli propaganda campaign when Hamas openly split from Syria, based on Damascus' repression against the popular uprising. And while some commentators attempted to equate the militancy and past use of armed resistance (some of which, in targeting civilians inside Israel, had indeed violated international law) to Israel's occupation with the brutal extremism of ISIS, the claimed linkage could not hold. The popularly elected Palestinian party that governs the still-occupied Gaza Strip continues to maintain ties with the now-outlawed Muslim Brotherhood in Egypt and the government of Qatar, not the extremists of ISIS or al-Qaeda.

Across the region as the 2010-11 Arab Spring erupted, many in the US and elsewhere in the West claimed that the core demands' focus on jobs and dignity somehow meant that the people of the Arab world no longer cared about Palestine and about Israeli occupation. But they were wrong. While the uprisings – and each had its own national particularities – shared a priority commitment to democracy, the rights of citizenship, and the basics of economic, social and political rights, there is no question that just barely beneath the surface, support for Palestinian rights and outrage at Israeli treatment of Palestinians remained intense.

For many, in the Arab world and beyond, the issue of double standards also erupted powerfully in the connection between the Syrian civil war, the war on terror and Israel's oppression of the Palestinians, particularly in Gaza. In August 2014, when President Obama talked about the urgent need to protect the Yazidi Kurds on Mount Sinjar, he described them as 'innocent people facing violence on a massive scale'. That was certainly true. And across the region many people also recognized the people of Gaza – where Israel had just carried out a 50-day military onslaught that left almost 2,200 people dead – as '1.8 million innocent people facing violence on a massive scale'. Many wondered why the US wasn't sending an airlift to overcome Israel's siege of Gaza, to force open Gaza's sealed border crossings and allow the people to escape their crowded, desperate enclave.

7 Looking forward

Isn't military force necessary against such a violent force as ISIS? What are the alternatives to war with ISIS?

President Obama was right when he said there is no military solution to the ISIS crisis. His decisions to bomb Syria, to return US troops to fight in Iraq and to send special forces to Syria, contradict that recognition. They also violate Obama's own commitment, made in his State of the Union address of 2014, to reverse Washington's 'perpetual war footing'. Instead, his renewal of a direct US military role in the region in the context of the rise of ISIS only makes that crisis worse. It gives ISIS and its allies a new basis for recruitment, it encourages extremists in other countries to link to and emulate ISIS, it strengthens the repressive Syrian government, it undermines Syria's struggling nonviolent opposition movement, and it further consolidates the links between ISIS supporters in Syria and in Iraq.

There are limits to what any government – including the US, the most powerful country in the world – is actually capable of doing. When the actions taken on the ground are in fact doing more harm than good, the response to those actions must be based on reclaiming the Hippocratic Oath: first, do no harm. That means rejecting actions – bombing, drone strikes, arming opposition forces, renewed US troop deployments – that are making the crisis worse.

And around the world, including in the US, Britain, France and elsewhere, there is the need to create responses to ISIS (and other terrorist) recruiting that do not make that situation worse as well. President Obama himself acknowledged that 'engagement with communities can't be a cover for surveillance. It can't securitize our relationship with Muslim Americans, dealing with them solely through the prism of law enforcement'. But he didn't do or even propose anything to actually change the US and local state and municipal policies that do just that. He made the statement at a White House conference designed to figure out how to counter recruiting by ISIS and similar organizations. But it wasn't held until mid-February 2015, a full seven months after Obama ordered the bombing to begin. In the meantime, a policy that depended precisely on using 'engagement with communities' as a 'cover for surveillance' and a law-enforcement-based 'securitized relationship with Muslim Americans' remained in effect. Prioritizing the law-enforcement response at home remained the parallel to prioritizing the military response in Syria, Iraq, Afghanistan, and beyond.

A month earlier, meeting with British Prime Minister David Cameron at the White House, President Obama described the 'phenomenon of violent extremism', saying: 'I do not consider it an existential threat.' Unlike the British leader, Obama did not use the term 'Islamic extremism'. He noted it was 'important for Europe not to simply respond with a hammer and law enforcement and military approaches to these problems', but he did not indicate then, or at the conference later, anything he would actually do to stop the reliance on precisely those approaches in his own country.

At the end of January 2015 the *New York Times* editorial board wrote: 'American officials see an emerging international consensus on the need for a long-term diplomatic solution between Mr Assad and diverse rebel groups. There is also interest in United Nations-led ceasefires in local communities like Aleppo that might serve as a basis for a broader peace… But it's unclear how plausible any of the ideas are, and no-one seems to have figured out how to tie these disparate pieces into a coherent game plan.' In fact it remained unclear just who in Washington, let alone in the rest of the world, actually believed there was an emerging consensus on anything regarding Syria diplomacy – and as long as that was the case, US reliance on military instead of diplomatic solutions would continue to carry the day.

When it comes to dealing with US policy toward ISIS, there are two critical understandings. One requires rejecting George W Bush's post-9/11 claim that the only choice was 'we either go to war, or we let 'em get away with it.' That was not the only choice for dealing with al-Qaeda then; it is not the only choice for dealing with ISIS now. War or nothing is never the only choice.

The other understanding means recognizing that there is often no strategy, no tactic that will successfully end an immediate attack, or resolve another kind of crisis, without causing much greater harm in the medium and long term. Whether or not military action is appropriate or legitimate is not dependent solely on how violent the potential target is. There are critical questions of law – international as well as domestic. There are questions of efficacy – will it work, will it make the threat go away or actually enable the threat to grow? There are challenging questions of consequence – what will happen, and who will come to power the day after? And there are the crucial questions of morality – when we know so many more people will die as a result of anticipated actions, how can we justify carrying them out? And of hypocrisy – when one country's actions have already been so culpable in creating a crisis, how dare that same government claim legitimacy in choosing to kill again, to destroy again, in the name of solving the crisis?

No US military action will result in ISIS immediately disappearing. And even if US or allied airstrikes manage to get the right target sometimes, and take out a rocket launcher or kill a truckload of ISIS fighters or destroy a house where an ISIS commander lives, the inevitability remains of family members being killed, of local anger being stoked, of homes and villages and whole cities being wiped out, of more people beginning to sympathize with violent extremists. All of this undermines any potential immediate military value. That was also true when Russia began bombing in Syria at the end of September 2015. While claiming its primary targets were ISIS, many civilians were killed and injured by Russian bombing raids that appeared to be targeting a range of anti-Assad opposition forces, including the al Qaeda-linked Nusra Front and others.

In July 2015 news broke that some of the airstrikes in Syria were flown by British pilots embedded with US, French and Canadian forces, despite the British Parliament's 2013 vote against military action in Syria. MPs challenged this in October and were assured that British pilots are no longer operating in Syria. However, also in October, there were widespread press reports that British pilots had been authorized to shoot down Russian warplanes if engaged by them over Iraq; the Russian government called in British diplomats to explain reports (denied by British officials) that British warplanes were being fitted with air-to-air munitions. In November 2015, the Cameron government dropped plans for a new parliamentary vote to approve air strikes in Syria, realizing that it again risked being defeated.

Arming the so-called moderate opposition in Syria doesn't mean the US is supporting the good guys. It means sending arms to the Free Syrian Army – and thus risking the almost inevitable result that the weapons will be expropriated by far more powerful violent extremists. It also means supporting FSA fighters who themselves, according to the *New York Times*, 'went on to behead six ISIS fighters... and then posted the photographs on Facebook' shortly after ISIS beheaded the US journalist James Foley.

In Syria, the CIA- and Pentagon-run programmes to vet and train thousands of new anti-ISIS fighters (the same ones who were going to be trained to fight against Assad) meant creating an entirely new US proxy army, almost certainly with little or no indigenous legitimacy. The Pentagon spent $500 million to train just 120 fighters, half of whom immediately defected, turning arms over to al Qaeda-linked and other extremist militias, and most of the other half were quickly defeated – leaving, in the words of the chief of US Central Command testifying before Congress in September 2015, 'a small number... we're talking four or five.' In Iraq, arming the Iraqi government and its allied militias doesn't solve the problem there. It means supporting a sectarian, Shi'a-dominated government in Baghdad, backed by even more sectarian militias, both responsible for terrible violence against Sunni communities. These policies continue to fail.

The US went to war in Afghanistan seeking revenge for the September 11 attacks. Britain joined the coalition to support the US call for vengeance. Years later, Jordan sent waves of airstrikes over Syria to avenge the killing of its bomber pilot. Japan's premier vowed revenge for ISIS killing two Japanese citizens in Syria. But while a military strike might bring some immediate public satisfaction, revenge is a dangerous basis for foreign policy.

Military attacks are wrong in a host of ways. Most are illegal under international law, immoral because of civilian casualties, and a distraction from vitally needed diplomacy. They also make real solutions impossible.

So what do serious alternatives to military solutions look like? To start with, we must recall why ISIS is so powerful in the first place.

ISIS has good weapons. Since 2011, the post-Qadafi chaos in Libya has brought a new flood of arms to a region already awash in weapons – mostly US-supplied and acquired directly or through Saudi Arabia and other Gulf states – for more than 15 years. So there needs to be a strategy of how to achieve a real arms embargo on all sides.

ISIS also has good military leadership. In Iraq, Sunni Ba'athist generals who were kicked out of their positions in the military when the US invaded are now providing training, strategy and military leadership to ISIS-allied militias and ISIS itself. Many of them reject religious extremism, and would be unlikely to continue support for ISIS if they believed a new, truly inclusive government in Iraq would give them some chance of recovering their lost jobs, prestige and dignity. It was not enough to elect a new prime minister in 2014 who speaks in more inclusive language, but announces a new government made up of too many of the same old sectarian faces. There needs to be a real strategy to convince those former military leaders that there is a place for them in a new and different Iraq.

ISIS draws additional strength from the support it receives from Sunni tribal leaders in Iraq – the very people President Obama says he wants to 'persuade' to break with ISIS. But these people are loyal to ISIS because, first during the US invasion and especially in the years of the US-backed Shi'a-controlled sectarian government of Nuri al-Maliki, they have suffered grievously. They were demonized, attacked and dispossessed by the government in Baghdad, and many of them see ISIS as the only possible ally and protector of Sunni interests, with the potential to challenge that government. These are often the same people who control large and powerful militias willing to fight alongside ISIS against the government in Baghdad. Clearly what's needed is an entirely new, inclusive political culture to replace Iraq's toxic sectarian divides.

ISIS also has the support of many ordinary Iraqi Sunnis. This largely secular constituency may hate what ISIS stands for, its religious extremism and violence, but, having faced arrest, torture, and extra-judicial execution under successive US-backed sectarian Shi'a-controlled national governments, many often choose to stand with ISIS against Baghdad. The Iraqi populace, especially Sunnis, must be convinced that the new government in Iraq really represents a break with the anti-Sunni sectarianism of the past to reverse the escalation of violence.

Ending the support that ISIS relies on from tribal leaders, military figures and ordinary Sunnis requires local mobilization, not US intervention. Washington needs to be pressed to acknowledge the limitations imposed by its damaged legitimacy and credibility. There are, however, many things that the US – some of them with the UK and others – can and must do to help end the brutal violence spreading across the Middle East.

Step 1: Remembering that doing no harm must be the top priority, the first step is to stop the airstrikes. Because while some in the US or UK may respond with 'Hooray, we got the bad guys', to many in Iraq (especially the very Sunnis President Obama wants to persuade to break with ISIS) the bombings and drone strikes appear to be the US acting as the air force of the Kurds and the Shi'a against the Sunnis. Rather than undermining popular support for ISIS, the airstrikes actually serve to strengthen the extremist organization.

Step 2: Make real the commitment to 'no boots on the ground' and withdraw the troops. After withdrawing all the US forces in 2011, the White House has authorized two deployments in 2014, sending a total of more than 3,500 troops back to Iraq, as well as a team of special forces publicly sent to Syria in October 2015. No-one knows how many unacknowledged pairs of CIA and JSOC (special operations forces) sneakers may also already be on the ground in Iraq or Syria. The presence of US troops provides exactly what ISIS and other extremist organizations want: US troops on their territory, providing potential recruits with renewed evidence of US meddling in Muslim countries, as well as providing thousands of new targets. This is identical to al-Qaeda's goal of 15 years ago, which was to provoke US troops into returning to their territory in order to fight them there.

Step 3: The US and its allies must stop flooding the region with arms. The weapons always seem to wind up in extremists' hands. The US-supplied Syrian 'moderates' too often are overrun by (or their fighters defect to) ISIS, al-Qaeda's Syrian franchise, or other not-so-moderate militias. And when Iraqi army generals abandon their troops, those forces in turn abandon their weapons and flee when faced with even small numbers of ISIS fighters. Whether these weapons are deployed by extremists or by the US-backed supposedly 'moderate' governments or militias, the result is more and more violence against civilians. Washington must end its policy of ignoring the violations of human rights and international law committed with its weapons and by its allies. Consistent enforcement of the Leahy Law prohibiting assistance to any foreign military units known to violate human rights must be an urgent demand. Only when the US stops providing weapons to its regional allies, who are arming the whole range of opposition forces from the Free Syrian Army to the most extreme Islamists, will Washington have the credibility to urge Iran and Russia to end their arming of the Syrian regime.

Step 4: The US should change its laws to reverse *Holder v. Humanitarian Law Project*, the Supreme Court decision that criminalizes as 'material support for terrorism' the teaching of nonviolence training, conflict resolution or how to access the United Nations human rights system, to any organization on Washington's list of 'foreign terrorist organizations'. That prohibition undermines any effort to win people in those organizations away from violence by providing information about nonviolent alternatives. The US should end its prohibitions on virtually any kind of contact with those listed as 'foreign terrorist organizations', including many in Syria and elsewhere in the region. The politicization of the list is a huge problem. This was evident in 2014 when the US resisted talking with or even acknowledging that the central players in saving the Yazidis besieged on Mount Sinjar were from a Kurdish militia in Syria allied with the PKK (Kurdistan Workers Party). The PKK had remained on the US anti-terrorism list so no US contact was allowed, even while the Turkish government was negotiating directly with them.

Step 5: There must be a real diplomatic partnership

to respond to the ISIS crisis. The US, many of its allies, and Russia are carrying out airstrikes and deploying new troops supposedly against ISIS in Iraq and Syria even while top US officials and much of the rest of the world agree there is no military solution. Diplomacy must be returned to centre stage. That means serious US engagement with Iran, among other players. Tehran has more influence in Baghdad than Washington does. Any serious effort to encourage Iraqi government acceptance of a truly inclusive approach to power will require joint pressure from the US and Iran. Even though Iran is predominantly Shi'a itself and its government claims global leadership of Shi'a Islam, the country's leaders are very worried about the instability in their next-door neighbour resulting from the years of Shi'a sectarianism in Baghdad. So there is every reason to anticipate Iranian support for damping down the sectarian-based violence in Iraq. The US-Iran nuclear agreement should form the basis for broadened talks toward a real 'grand bargain' between the US and Iran to include all the related crises, including normalization of Iran's role in the region. The November 2015 talks initiated by the US and Russia, with Iran participating for the first time along with Washington's regional allies, hold some hope for movement towards a diplomatic solution to the ISIS crisis. Those talks could lead to the US and Iran jointly pushing for an end to anti-Sunni sectarianism in the Iraqi government, and, in collaboration with Russia, jointly working toward ending the multi-party civil war in Syria.

Step 6: The US should support a new search for broader diplomatic solutions in the United Nations involving both ISIS and the civil war in Syria. The November 2015 talks in Vienna could pave the way for such a UN initiative, particularly since the joint statement of the outside powers backing the main players in Syria specifically 'invited the UN to convene representatives of the Government of Syria and the Syrian opposition for a political process leading to credible, inclusive, non-sectarian governance, followed by a new constitution and elections.' One aspect should be greater support for UN efforts to negotiate local ceasefires in Syria. Those efforts, renewed in Aleppo in early March 2015, have led to important examples of encouraging short-term truces to create humanitarian corridors and allow humanitarian aid into and evacuation of civilians from besieged areas. The Vienna statement eight months later recognized the need for an even broader ceasefire, noting 'the participants together with the United Nations will explore modalities for, and implementation of, a nationwide ceasefire to be initiated on a date certain and in parallel with this renewed political process.'

That doesn't necessarily mean calling for the opening of direct talks with ISIS – that is neither practically nor politically viable in the short term. It does mean working to build a real coalition aimed at changing the desperate conditions that lead ordinary people, people with power and without power, to consider supporting ISIS.

Eventually, even talks with ISIS should not be permanently ruled out. Jonathan Powell, former chief of staff for then-prime minister and Iraq war supporter Tony Blair, reminded CNN in October 2014:

People forget how long the process leading up to a successful negotiation can take. The British government opened up a secret channel to the IRA in 1972 and yet the real negotiations only happened in 1991-93 when [then UK prime minister John] Major opened his correspondence with Irish republican politician Martin McGuinness. It takes a long time for armed groups to realize that their demands are unachievable and to start to consider what else they would settle for.

The same is true of ISIS. No-one is going to agree to a universal caliphate. But once ISIS realizes they can't win then they may be prepared to talk and we need to open a secret channel now to give time to establish enough trust to move to negotiations when the moment comes. There are practical things we can talk to them about. The ex-Baathists and ex-Iraqi army officers that make up a major part of the ISIS force have genuine grievances about the way they were treated by the sectarian Maliki government. We can discuss with them ways of ensuring Sunnis have a powerful voice in a Shi'a-majority Iraq.

A viable international coalition will require replacing military strikes with powerful diplomacy. The US will have to pressure its ally Saudi Arabia to stop arming and financing ISIS and other extremist fighters; pressure its ally Turkey to stop allowing ISIS and other fighters to cross into Syria over the Turkish border; pressure its allies Qatar, Saudi Arabia, the UAE, Jordan and others to stop financing and arming everyone and anyone in Syria who says he or she is against Assad. What is *not* needed is another Coalition of the Killing; what is needed instead is a newly created Coalition of the Rebuilding. Building on the success of the hard-won nuclear deal, shared opposition to ISIS can provide a new expansion of co-operation between the US and its long-time competitors Russia and Iran.

Step 7: Push the United Nations, despite the resignation of special envoys in 2012 and 2014, to restart real negotiations on ending the civil war in Syria. Eventually that means everyone involved needs to be at the table: the Syrian regime; civil society inside Syria including nonviolent activists, women, young people, internally displaced, and refugees forced to flee Syria (Syrian, Iraqi, and Palestinian); the Syrian Kurds, Christians, Druze, and other minorities as well as Sunnis, Shi'a, and Alawites; the armed rebels; the external opposition and the regional and global players supporting all sides – the US, Russia, Iran, Saudi Arabia, the UAE, Qatar, Turkey, Jordan, Lebanon and beyond.

This could provide a moment for the US to collaborate with Russia on Syria policy, building on the successful joint effort to destroy Syria's chemical weapons and perhaps lessening tensions over Ukraine. A ceasefire and arms embargo on all sides should be the medium-term goal – which will only be possible if the US is prepared to exert serious pressure on its allies to stop arming all their favourite factions, even as pressure is brought to bear on Iran and Russia to stop the flow of arms to the Syrian government.

It should not be forgotten that despite initial US reluctance to send arms directly to the rebels, their weapons are mostly US-produced, having been sold to Washington's allied Gulf monarchies over the years in multi-billion-dollar arms deals. (Britain and France have sold weapons to Gulf states as well.) All US and UK weapons sold internationally, including to close allies, contain end-use restrictions limiting how they can be used, and whether and to whom they can be resold – though these are rarely applied in practice. There is little doubt that the US could, if it chose, bring an immediate halt to the Saudi, UAE, Qatari and other arms shipments heading to the Syrian opposition forces by enforcing those end-use restrictions, on pain of losing all future access to US arms.

Step 8: The US must be pushed to massively increase its humanitarian contributions to United Nations agencies for the millions of refugees and internally displaced people both inside and fleeing from both Syria and Iraq. Money is desperately needed both inside Syria and in the surrounding countries where millions of Syrians have sought refuge. The US has pledged significant funds, but much of it has not actually been made available to the agencies, and more must be pledged and given.

What can people – separate from governments – do to help end the wars and support movements for freedom and liberation in the Middle East?

The most important thing activists can do is to build movements that challenge the prevailing war policies of their own governments, that raise the political price at home for going to war abroad. That work takes the form of education, advocacy, and protest. The goal is no less than to transform government policy – from one based on military responses to crises that demand non-military solutions to a policy based on diplomacy, humanitarian assistance, negotiations, and international-law-based alternatives. And that means ending the political and strategic support Washington relies on from its allies in London and beyond.

In the US, it means reminding people about both the global and the US-specific histories of challenging militarism, war profiteering, and violence. The fourth of Franklin D Roosevelt's 'four freedoms', for instance, speaks of the 'freedom from fear which, translated into world terms, means a worldwide reduction of armaments to such a point and in such a thorough fashion that no nation will be in a position to commit an act of physical aggression against any neighbor – anywhere in the world.' And whether FDR would have described it so or not, for those in the US today, that means starting with the worldwide reduction of *US* armaments. In Britain, France, Australia, Canada and other countries whose governments have backed US war efforts, similar campaigns to reduce arms sales and replace military policies with strengthened diplomacy are needed.

To accomplish those terribly difficult goals will require anti-war mobilization that engages with people in far greater numbers and far broader politics than those who define themselves as against war or pro peace. It will require inserting opposition to war and to militarism into the very centre of every effort under way, every social movement fighting for human rights, for people and the planet, for people over profits, for justice.

Education

At the educational level that requires a campaign to debunk the myth, powerfully propagated by George W

Bush on 12 September 2001, the day after the terror attacks in the US, that the only choice is to 'either go to war, or let 'em get away with it'. Non-military alternatives – diplomacy, negotiations, multilateral co-operation – must be reclaimed as the first choice, the default choice – rejecting the current habit of mentioning non-military solutions only as an afterthought, and only after the military attacks begin. That means providing people with the resources to understand what those non-military solutions are.

There must be a willingness to challenge claims such as 'you can't use diplomacy, ISIS would never talk.' The answer includes understanding that, first, some kind of diplomacy is always necessary. Second, it need not start with talking to ISIS directly, but by negotiating initially with those who provide ISIS with the weapons and money to keep fighting, those responsible for creating the conditions that lead some people to support ISIS, or those others who justify the brutality of ISIS or related groups. It also means recognizing that some negotiations in Syria have already gone forward between fighters at the local level with the goal of establishing local ceasefires, and there may well come a time when ISIS fighters, with or without their leadership, would participate in such talks as well. (See 'Isn't military force necessary?' for more on how negotiations with ISIS might occur.)

There must be education about the origins of ISIS and its predecessor organizations – how they arose as part of the response to the US/UK invasion and occupation of Iraq. That means teaching and discussing the legacy of US interrogation and torture at Abu Ghraib and Guantánamo, and the consequences of US detention of so many tens of thousands of Iraqis and others during the war, without trial, without rights, without justice. Assessments of military and intelligence officials regarding the lack of efficacy of torture strengthen moral and international law arguments. In 2006, for example, the former head of US Army intelligence, General John

Kimmons, admitted: 'no good intelligence is going to come from abusive practices. I think history tells us that. I think the empirical evidence of the last five years, hard years, tells us that.'

There must be solid education about what ISIS is and isn't – not to defend or justify its violence, but precisely the opposite: because understanding what motivates such brutality is crucial to stopping it. That may mean learning something about the theological framework that defines the organization, including its roots in Saudi Arabia's Wahhabi form of Islam. But even more important than the religious details, it means learning about why a wide range of people, including many who may be novices in Islamic practice or not even Muslim at all, but who share a powerful sense of individual or collective alienation, of bitter dislocation, of utter hopelessness in their home community or country, end up supporting ISIS. Muslim activists, including religious leaders and Muslims of all degrees of devoutness, who overwhelmingly oppose ISIS and are already playing a huge role in confronting the effect of those challenges in their community, must be supported.

Education and advocacy on Israeli occupation and apartheid, on Palestinian rights and international law, must be continued. While the question of Palestine and US support for Israel are not necessarily at the centre of popular debate and discussion across the region now defined as a US 'war zone', those issues remain central to public consciousness. They are at the core of opposition to US intervention and the widespread delegitimation of US-backed Arab leaders.

Writing letters to the editor in local papers; calling in to talk shows on local radio stations; arranging meetings with editorial boards of local newspapers: all of these can play important roles in educating broader parts of the public. And if a letter to the editor contains the name of a local politician, the letter helps play an advocacy role as well, since politicians' staff are generally rigorous in tracking anything in print or online mentioning their boss.

The situation in the Middle East and the destabilizing role of the US wars there is certainly complicated. But there are plenty of good resources available – books, films, speakers, online resources – that are useful for study groups, education programmes, and individual engagement. Many are included in the resource list at the back of this book. Sharing with family, friends, and co-workers is always a good place to start.

Advocacy

The most effective advocacy work comes through collective rather than individual action. So joining existing peace and anti-war organizations, forming anti-militarism and peace contingents within broader campaigns for justice, seeking out like-minded individuals within trade unions, faith-based communities, schools and universities, community and political organizations always provides the best potential. Anti-war and peace organizations are neighbourhood or city-based, statewide or national, and often global. Advocacy with governments means direct contact with politicians, including bird-dogging them at town meetings and public events, insisting they answer questions about their support for war, or thanking them for their opposition. Initiating and signing petitions is always useful – sign them all, then follow up with direct contact. Even better, send an individual letter, by fax or snail mail, saying the same thing – the individual effort makes it more important. Better still, call your member of Congress or Parliament to register your concerns. And best of all, request meetings with members or their staff, perhaps when the members are home in their district during recess periods. These are the most effective opportunities for constituents to urge their representatives to hear their arguments.

Contacting members of Congress or Parliament sometimes seems fruitless. But it is important to remember that individual members still have to get the votes every few years to stay in office. That means they can be reached more often than is sometimes apparent – especially by their own constituents. On the question of the US war on terror, there is a potent pro-war influence from key lobbies, including the pro-Israel lobby and most of all the powerful arms manufacturers' lobby. Anti-war organizers can't compete with those wealthy political forces dollar for dollar, but exposing and delegitimizing their influence on Congress is a key component of opposing war.

In some instances advocacy can be strengthened through sectoral relationships built between con-stituency-based organizations in the US or UK and their counterparts in the war zones. One powerful example has been the decade-long ties built between US Labor Against the War and the Iraqi Oil Workers Union. Bringing out the voices of people who are the targets of US wars and interventions is crucial to humanizing whole populations who otherwise tend to be lumped into stereotyped images of either 'terrorists' or 'victims' – not people with their own agency, with families and communities, with dreams and ideas. Another example is the work of Iraq Veterans Against the War in the US and Veterans for Peace UK, whose members continue to partner with various Afghan and Iraqi organizations on campaigns including the demand for reparations in Iraq and better access to medical care for both Iraqi civilians and US and British veterans of the war.

Protest campaigns
Politicians who posture about the importance of political solutions while launching military strikes that undermine those same political solutions, and then ignoring political alternatives altogether, must be consistently called out for their hypocrisy.

There is a need for continuing protests against the US-led wars. In recent years, as the number of ground troops has been reduced and replaced by an escalating drone and special-forces war, public attention in the US has waned. Keeping the public focused on the wars remains a crucial starting point to building opposition to them.

That includes reminding the public of the costs of war – in the US, for example, the 2015 announcement that the Obama administration's war against ISIS would cost $5.8 billion just for the next year should, for example, be at the front and centre of campaigns. It can be made more real by linking that cost to possible alternative uses of that $5.8 billion of tax money – in job creation, healthcare, education, infrastructure, or perhaps in helping to rebuild the countries US wars have so damaged. Similar tradeoff campaigns might target the $10.54 million that US taxpayers have been paying for the war on terror *every hour* since 2001. Or the more than *half a trillion* dollars in 2014 to fund the Department of Defense, an amount that does not include the tens of billions for fighting the actual wars or for maintaining the US nuclear weapons arsenal on high alert – for just one year.

Protest campaigns may or may not choose public demonstrations at any given moment. When education about the costs – human, economic, international law, human rights, environmental – has been effective, when anti-war ideas are popular and strong, protests in the streets are an unsurpassed, vital component of anti-war activism. When a street protest is likely to appear small and marginal, sometimes a return to educational campaigning may be more appropriate.

In the UK as in the US, there is a need for constant campaigns, educational and protest-based, against Islamophobia, making clear that much of the traditional law-enforcement-based strategy for identifying and dealing with potential terrorists is not only failing to solve the problem of ISIS recruitment but also antagonizing whole populations through illegal surveillance, discriminatory arrests and prosecution, racial and religious profiling. Understanding that much of the domestic strategy targeting Arab and Muslim communities is thoroughly linked to carrying out the wars abroad, organizations working primarily against Islamophobia and anti-Arab racism and those based in the communities most affected must be included at the centre of anti-war organizing.

Movements against war must be international and internationalist. That means building and maintaining ties with anti-war campaigners around the world, including, though not limited to, counterparts in countries whose governments, often in opposition to massive public opinion, are allied members of the US war coalition. It also means working to give voice to those living the consequences of the US strategy – those whose families have been killed or injured by US airstrikes, drones, bombs, or soldiers; those forced to flee their homes as a result of US-involved fighting; those unable to find work or feed their children because of US policies that have devastated their countries and their economies. And it means working within broader campaigns for justice to help consolidate internationalism as a core value and core organizing principle of every social movement mobilizing to change the world.

Anti-war organizing will never succeed when it is limited to self-defined anti-war or peace organizations. Only when anti-war, anti-militarism, anti-military-spending themes emerge as one stream in the much wider river of campaigns for racial, economic, social, environmental justice, and human rights will social movements working to end wars be able to claim victory.

Postscript

As this book went to press, the terrorist attacks on Paris took place on 13 November 2015. That night, Phyllis Bennis contributed her own immediate response to the website of The Nation.

After the Paris attacks, a call for justice, not vengeance

France is in mourning and in shock. We still don't know how many people were killed and injured. In fact, there's a lot we still don't know – including who was responsible. The ISIS claim of responsibility tells us virtually nothing about who really planned or carried out the attacks; opportunist claims are an old story. But the lack of information hasn't prevented lots of assumptions about who is 'obviously' responsible and what should be done to them. Already the call is rising across France – 'this time it's all-out war'.

But we do know what happens when cries of war and vengeance drown out all other voices; we've heard them before.

A few days after the 9/11 attacks, we at the Institute for Policy Studies and some of our allies organized a public statement whose lead signatories included Harry Belafonte, Danny Glover, Gloria Steinem, Rosa Parks, and many more. The statement reflected the deeply rooted fear we all shared, that however horrific the attacks of September 11, it was George W Bush's statement in response to those attacks that threatened the world. That was the moment he announced that the response to this enormous crime against humanity would be a war – that he would lead the world to war 'against terror'.

We know how that played out. It didn't work out so well. Already we're hearing French officials and commentators and pundits calling for more of the same.

'This time it's all-out war' is the French version of Bush's 'you're either with us or with the terrorists'.

But wars of vengeance won't work for France any more than they worked for the United States.

The public statement we issued back in 2001 was a call for 'Justice, Not Vengeance'. It began:

Our hearts and prayers go out in compassion to the victims and their families who have suffered so greatly from the unspeakable acts of brutality committed on September 11, 2001.

We share the shock, anger, and grief of so many people in the US and around the world and call for a response that is prompt, just, and effective. We foresee that a military response would not end the terror. Rather, it would spark a cycle of escalating violence, the loss of innocent lives, and new acts of terrorism. As citizens of this great nation, we support the efforts being made to find those behind the acts of terror. Bringing them to justice under the rule of law – not military action – is the way to end the violence.

We note that although the terrorist acts of September 11 were aimed at the United States, citizens of over 50 nations are counted among the victims. The carnage of terrorism knows no borders. Our best chance for preventing such devastating acts of terror is to act decisively and co-operatively as part of a community of nations within the framework of international law to root out terrorism and work for justice at home and abroad.

We affirm that the United States is a nation of laws, rooted in fundamental American values of democracy, justice, human rights, and respect for life. The laws that protect our civil liberties and freedoms in the United States are part of what define us as a nation. They must not be abridged; to do so would offer victory to those who wrought these vengeful acts.

But those laws, the laws rooted in 'democracy, justice, human rights and respect for life' were, of course, abridged. Worse than abridged, they were crushed – by torture at Bagram and Abu Ghraib and Guantánamo Bay, and by airstrikes and drone attacks that killed scores of Afghan, Iraqi, Pakistani, Yemeni, Somali, or other civilians for every alleged bad guy they took aim at. The laws were sidelined by racial profiling and round-ups of Muslims and Arabs and Arab-Americans, violated by NSA spying on a scale so massive as to be virtually unfathomable, ignored by craven members of Congress content to allow presidents unlimited funds to wage unilateral wars.

There was another possible response, the one reflected in the French newspaper *Le Monde* just hours after the 9/11 attacks. 'Nous sommes tous Américains,' the headline read. We are all Americans now. It was a sentiment reflected in candlelight vigils, in handwritten letters, in the human solidarity of crowds pouring into the streets from Tehran to Tokyo. And it was squandered by the wars that followed – the wars for which Bush told the world and lied to Americans with the claim that the choice was to either go to war, or 'let 'em get away with it'. And since no-one wanted to let 'them' get away with such a heinous crime, a vast majority of the American people supported war. At first. But then, as a powerful anti-war movement rose, more people began to see, to understand, the cost – human, economic, environmental, legal, diplomatic, and beyond – of these wars, and their failure to achieve any of the powerful goals we were assured they would accomplish.

Because now everyone knows the devastating wars that killed so many hundreds of thousands of ordinary people didn't work to wipe out terrorism. Terrorism survives wars; people don't. We saw the proof of that again last night in Paris, and we saw it the day before in Beirut. We were hearing sounds of victory from US war-makers. The Obama strategy was working, they said. ISIS was being pushed back from Sinjar by Kurdish militias. A US airstrike assassinated Mohammed Emwasi, known as 'Jihadi John' from the ISIS videos. Yet the war – a new version of that same 'global war on terror'

– is still being waged, and clearly it still isn't working. Because you can't bomb terrorism – you can only bomb people. You can bomb cities. Sometimes you might kill a terrorist – but that doesn't end terrorism; it only encourages more of it.

It didn't have to be that way. A day or so after the 9/11 attacks, we at the IPS received a message from a colleague of ours, the great Bolivian water-rights activist Oscar Olivera. 'We still believe another world is possible,' he wrote. 'We are with you.' Global solidarity with us – with Americans – was real. No longer, not since our government took the world to war.

It doesn't have to be that way in Paris. It isn't too late. 'We stand with Paris' is our cry today – as 'Nous sommes tous Américains' was the cry of our French comrades 15 years ago. Maybe they can get it right.

Resources

Peace and Anti-War Organizations

September Eleventh Families for Peaceful Tomorrows
peacefultomorrows.org

Alternatives (Canada)
alternatives.ca

American Friends Service Committee afsc.org

Bertrand Russell Peace Foundation
russfound.com

Campaign Against Arms Trade
caat.org.uk

Campaign for Nuclear Disarmament cnduk.org

Canadian Peace Alliance
canadianpeace.org

Center for Constitutional Rights
ccrjustice.org

Coalition to Oppose the Arms Trade (Canada) coat.ncf.ca

Code Pink codepink.org

Drone Wars UK dronewars.net

European Network Against Arms Trade enaat.org

Fellowship of Reconciliation
for.org.uk

Friends Committee on National Legislation fcnl.org

Historians Against the War
historiansagainstwar.org

Institute for Policy Studies
ips-dc.org

Inter-Pares interpares.ca

Iraq Veterans Against the War
ivaw.org

Jewish Voice for Peace
jewishvoiceforpeace.org

Just Foreign Policy
justforeignpolicy.org

Military Families Speak Out
mfso.org

Muslim Association of Britain
mabonline.net

National Lawyers Guild nlg.org

Palestine Solidarity Campaign
palestinecampaign.org

Pax Christi paxchristiusa.org

Peace Action peace-action.org

Peace Pledge Union ppu.org.uk

People's Assembly Against Austerity
thepeoplesassembly.org.uk

Quaker Peace and Disarmament Programme quaker.org.uk

Saferworld saferworld.org.uk

Stockholm International Peace Research Institute sipri.org

Stop the War Coalition
stopwar.org.uk

Transnational Institute tni.org

United for Peace & Justice
unitedforpeace.org

US Campaign to End the Israeli Occupation
endtheoccupation.org

US Labor Against the War
uslaboragainstwar.org

Veterans for Peace
veteransforpeace.org

War on Want   waronwant.org

War Resisters League
warresisters.org

Win Without War
winwithoutwar.org

Women's Action for New Directions wand.org

Women's International League for Peace and Freedom
wilpfinternational.org

Books

Eqbal Ahmad, *The Selected Writings of Eqbal Ahmad*, Columbia University Press, 2006.

Eqbal Ahmad, *Confronting Empire:*

Interviews With David Barsamian, South End Press, 2000.

Medea Benjamin, *Drone Warfare: Killing by Remote Control*, Verso, 2013.

Phyllis Bennis, *Before & After: US Foreign Policy and the War on Terror*, Olive Branch Press, 2002.

Phyllis Bennis, *Challenging Empire: How People, Governments and the UN Defy US Power*, Olive Branch Press, 2005.

Phyllis Bennis, *Ending the US War in Afghanistan: A Primer*, Olive Branch Press, 2010. Co-author David Wildman.

Phyllis Bennis, *Inside Israel-Palestine*, New Internationalist, 2010.

James Carroll, *House of War: The Pentagon and the Disastrous Rise of American Power*, Mariner Books, 2006.

Noam Chomsky, *Pirates and Emperors, Old and New: International Terrorism in the Real World*, South End Press, 2002.

Noam Chomsky, *Hegemony or Survival: America's Quest for Global Dominance*, Henry Holt, 2003.

Noam Chomsky, *Rogue States: The Rule of Force in World Affairs*, Pluto Press, 2000.

Patrick Cockburn, *The Jihadis Return*, OR Books, 2014.

Patrick Cockburn, *The Rise of Islamic State: ISIS and the New Sunni Revolution*, Verso, 2015.

Marjorie Cohn, *Cowboy Republic: Six Ways the Bush Gang Has Defied the Law*, PoliPointPress, 2007.

Marjorie Cohn, *Drones and Targeted Killing: Legal, Moral, and Geopolitical Issues*, Interlink Books, 2015.

Steve Coll, *Ghost Wars: The Secret History of the CIA, Afghanistan, and Bin Laden From the Soviet Invasion to September 10, 2001*, Penguin, 2004.

Robert Dreyfuss, *Devil's Game: How the United States Helped Unleash Fundamentalist Islam*, Metropolitan Books, 2005.

Richard Falk, *Humanitarian Intervention and Legitimacy Wars: Seeking Peace & Justice in the 21st Century*, Routledge, 2015.

Richard Falk, *Palestine: The Legitimacy of Hope*, Just World Books, 2014.

Jean-Pierre Filiu, *From Deep State to Islamic State*, Hurst, 2015.

Michael Griffin, *Islamic State – Rewriting History*, Pluto Press 2015.

Robert Jensen, *Citizens of the Empire: The Struggle to Claim Our Humanity*, City Lights, 2004.

Chalmers Johnson, *The Sorrows of Empire: Militarism, Secrecy, and the End of the Republic*, Metropolitan Books, 2005.

Rashid Khalidi, *Resurrecting Empire: Western Footprints and America's Perilous Path in the Middle East*, Beacon Press, 2005.

Michael T Klare, *Rising Powers, Shrinking Planet: The New Geopolitics of Energy*, Metropolitan Books, 2008.

Mahmood Mamdani, *Good Muslim, Bad Muslim: America, the Cold War, and the Roots of Terror*, Harmony Books, 2004.

Vijay Mehta, *The Economics of Killing: How the West Fuels War and Poverty in the Developing World*, Pluto Press, 2012.

Sami Moubayed, *Under the Black Flag*, IB Tauris, 2015.

Ahmed Rashid, *Descent Into Chaos: The United States and the Failure of Nation Building in Pakistan, Afghanistan, and Central Asia,* Penguin, 2008.

Ahmed Rashid, *Taliban: Militant Islam, Oil and Fundamentalism in Central Asia,* Yale University Press, 2001.

Thomas E Ricks, *Fiasco: The American Military Adventure in Iraq,* Penguin, 2006.

Jeremy Scahill, *Dirty Wars: The World Is a Battlefield,* Nation Books, 2013.

Anthony Shadid, *Night Draws Near: Iraq's People in the Shadow of America's War,* Picador, 2005.

Raja Shehadeh and Penny Johnson, eds, *Shifting Sands: the Unraveling of the Old Order in the Middle East,* Profile Books, 2015.

Müge Gürsöy Sökmen, ed, *World Tribunal on Iraq: Making the Case Against War,* Olive Branch Press, 2008.

Joseph E Stiglitz and Linda J Bilmes, *The Three Trillion Dollar War: The True Cost of the Iraq Conflict,* WW. Norton, 2008.

Achin Vanaik, ed, *Selling US Wars,* Olive Branch Press, 2007.

Reports

Afghanistan Index, Brookings Institution, Feb 2015, nin.tl/brookingsfeb15

Amy Belasco, 'The Cost of Iraq, Afghanistan and other Global War on Terror Operations Since 9/11,' Congressional Research Service Report for Congress, 8 Feb 2008, nin.tl/belascoreport

Phyllis Bennis, 'Alternatives to War: Eight Things the US Should do Regarding ISIS', Testimony for Briefing on ISIS and the Authorization for the US of Force, Progressive Caucus of the US Congress, 3 Mar 2015, nin.tl/bennistestimony

IPS and FPIF, 'The Iraq Quagmire: The Mounting Costs of the Iraq War', 31 Aug 2005, nin.tl/iraqquagmire

Open Society Justice Initiative, 'Death by Drone: Civilian Harm Caused by US Targeted Killings in Yemen', 14 Apr 2015, nin.tl/opensocietyjustice

Magazines and websites

Al-Jazeera aljazeera.net

AlterNet alternet.org

CommonDreams commondreams.org

Foreign Policy in Focus fpif.org

Ha'aretz (Israeli daily) haaretz.com

In These Times inthesetimes.org

Informed Comment on Middle East juancole.com

Institute for Policy Studies ips-dc.org

Iraq Body Count (UK) iraqbodycount.org

ISIS & Radicalization Resources du.edu/korbel/middleeast/isis. html

Middle East Report merip.org

The Nation thenation.com

New Internationalist newint.org

The Progressive theprogressive.org

Syria Comment joshualandis.com

Truthout truth-out.org

Index